Goin' Down De Mont
A People's History of Rock Concerts at Leicester's De Montfort Hall

Bruce Pegg

Spenwood Books
Manchester, UK

De Montfort Hall, Leicester — Ticket Stubs

Rory Gallagher	Mon. April 21, 7.30 p.m.	Stalls Standing	£1.10
Rory Gallagher	Thur. Nov. 22, 7.30 p.m.	Stalls (Standing)	£1.10
The Sensational Alex Harvey Band	Tues. May 20, 7.30 p.m.	Stalls Standing	£1.00
Man	Mon. Mar. 15, 7.30 p.m.	Standing	£1.00
The Sweet	Mon. June 18, 7.30 p.m.	Stalls Standing	75p
Leo Sayer	Tues. Sept. 17, 7.30 p.m.	Stalls Standing	75p
Mick Ronson	Sun. April 28, 8.00 p.m.	Stalls Standing	£1
Jo'Burg Hawk	Thur. May 24, 7.30 p.m.	Balcony	44p
Lynyrd Skynyrd plus support	Mon. Feb. 14, 7.30 p.m.	Gallery	£1.50
Nazareth (No Mean City Tour)	Tue. Jan. 30, 7.30 p.m.	Stalls Standing	£2.00
Blue Öyster Cult	Wed. April 26, 7.30 p.m.	Stalls Standing	£2.00
The Crawlers, Boxer and Moon	Thur. July 21, 7.30 p.m.	Balcony	£1.00
Wishbone Ash	Tues. Oct. 31, 8.00 p.m.	Stalls Standing	£2.00
Black Sabbath plus support	Wed. May 31, 7.30 p.m.	Stalls Standing	£1.75

Row 1

DE MONTFORT HALL, LEICESTER
Tony Smith for John Smith Entertainments on behalf of Leicester Corporation presents
BLACK SABBATH
STALLS
Standing
£1.25
including V.A.T.
Mon. Dec. 17
at 7.30 p.m.
152

DE MONTFORT HALL, LEICESTER
Tony Smith for John Smith Entertainments presents
T. REX
Sun. Jan. 27
at 7.30 p.m.
STALLS
£1.25
including VAT
Standing
69

De Montfort Hall, LEICESTER
Derek Block Concert Promotions present
HAWKWIND
Thur. Jan. 30
at 7.30 p.m.
STALLS
£1.10
INCLUDING VAT
STANDING
1369

DE MONTFORT HALL, LEICESTER
Derek Block in association with ASGARD
HAWKWIND
STALLS
£1.00
(STANDING)
including V.A.T.
Wed. Jan. 2
at 7.30 p.m.
564

Row 2

De Montfort Hall, Leicester
M.C.P. presents
JUDAS PRIEST
plus support
Mon. May 21   7.30 p.m.
STALLS
£2.50
INCLUDING VAT
Standing
818

De Montfort Hall, LEICESTER
John Smith Entertainments in Association with Bronze Records present
URIAH HEEP
plus PETER FRAMPTON
Tues. Oct. 29
at 7.30 p.m.
STALLS
£1.00
INCLUDING VAT
Standing
203

De Montfort Hall, LEICESTER
John Smith Entertainments present
URIAH HEEP
plus support
Wed. Dec. 3
at 7.30 p.m.
STALLS
Standing
£1.10
(including V.A.T.)
284

De Montfort Hall, LEICESTER
Derek Block presents
STATUS QUO
Fri. May 9
at 7.30 p.m.
STALLS
Standing
£1.50
including V.A.T.
098

Row 3

De Montfort Hall, LEICESTER
Harvey Goldsmith Entertainments present
RITCHIE BLACKMORE'S RAINBOW
Wed. Sept. 1
at 7.30 p.m.
STALLS
Standing
£1.50
(including V.A.T.)
109

De Montfort Hall, Leicester
Straight Music presents
U.F.O.
Mon. June 19
at 7.30 p.m.
STALLS   £1.50
(including V.A.T.)
Standing
0077

De Montfort Hall, Leicester
M.C.P. presents
JUDAS PRIEST
plus support
Mon. May 21   7.30 p.m.
STALLS
£2.50
INCLUDING VAT
Standing
819

De Montfort Hall, Leicester
Midland Concert Promotions present
JUDAS PRIEST
Fri. Nov. 3
at 7.30 p.m.
STALLS   £2.00
(including V.A.T.)
Standing
470

Row 4

De Montfort Hall, Leicester
Double M Concerts Ltd. present
IAN HUNTER'S OVERNIGHT ANGELS
Thur. June 9
at 7.30 p.m.
STALLS   £1.75
(including V.A.T.)
Standing
196

De Montfort Hall, Leicester
Mel Bush presents
RENAISSANCE
Fri. Sept. 22
at 8.00 p.m.
STALLS   £1.60
(including V.A.T.)
LL22

De Montfort Hall, Leicester
RALPH McTELL
Sat. May 12
at 7.30 p.m.
STALLS   £1.00
(including V.A.T.)
JJ23

First published in Great Britain 2022
by Spenwood Books Ltd
Paperback edition published 2023

2 College Street, Higham Ferrers, NN10 8DZ.

Copyright © Bruce Pegg 2022 & 2023

The right of Bruce Pegg to be identified
as author of this work has been asserted in
accordance with Section 77 of the Copyright,
Design and Patents Act 1988.

A CIP record for this book is available from the
British Library.

ISBN 978-1-9168896-4-4 (hardback)
ISBN 978-1-915858-20-7 (paperback)

Hardback printed and bound by Sound Performance Ltd,
3 Greenwich Quay, Clarence Road, Greenwich,
London, SE8 3EY.

Design by Bruce Graham, The Night Owl.
Front cover image: Robert Morris/Alamy stock photo
(De Montfort Hall); Mark Healey (Annie Lennox); Paul
Canny (Geddy Lee); John Chapman (Ozzy Osbourne).

Rear cover image: Alan Jones
All other image copyrights: As captioned.

GOIN' DOWN DE MONT: A PEOPLE'S HISTORY

ABOUT THE AUTHOR

A professional musician and music historian, Bruce Pegg currently works as a writer and editor. He is the author of *Brown Eyed Handsome Man: The Life and Hard Times of Chuck Berry* (Routledge, 2002), the definitive biography of the rock and roll pioneer, along with several critical essays about the musician. He also wrote the extensive liner notes that accompany *Rock and Roll Music: Any Old Way You Choose It*, Bear Family Records' comprehensive 16-CD collection of Berry's entire studio output and select live recordings.

Born and raised in Leicester, England, he currently resides in central New York. His writing about music, running, and spirituality can be found at brucepegg.com.

Before and after. The author in 1980 (wearing an original Genesis *Duke* tour t-shirt) and today. Courtesy Sarah McPherson (1980) and Richard Grant (2022)

ACKNOWLEDGEMENTS

Even though my name appears on the cover, this is not really my book. It truly belongs to everyone who contributed a story or an image. I would like to thank them all for helping this labour of love see the light of day.

I would also like to thank the almost 400 members of the *Goin' Down De Mont* Facebook group who also contributed stories, knowledge, images, suggestions and ideas that found their way into these pages in one way or another.

And while it would be unfair to single out individuals, I would like to acknowledge two people in particular who helped enormously while I put the book together. The first is my old friend Glenn Williams, who was quick to answer all my questions and fill the gaps in my memory and research. The second is Richard Houghton, who not only came up with the idea for the book but who also provided encouragement as I was writing it and patiently and painstakingly saw the book through the publication process. Thanks to him, and designer Bruce Graham, this book has become a fitting tribute to the De Mont.

Last, I want to thank my Mum and Dad, who trusted me all those years ago with the precious gift of freedom, allowing me to see my heroes – even on a school night – without ever denying me the opportunity while never fully understanding why goin' down De Mont meant so much to me.

This book is dedicated to Joan and Dick's grandkids – William, Carolyn and Hannah Pegg. I hope it somehow helps explain how their Dad's love for music began and eventually found its way into their genes.

Bruce Pegg
Cazenovia, New York
September 2022

GOIN' DOWN DE MONT: A PEOPLE'S HISTORY

CONTENTS

Foreword 7

Introduction 9

The Fifties 21

The Sixties 22

The Seventies 46

The Eighties 119

The Nineties & Beyond 172

Afterword 191

Discography 192

Gigography 199

Special Thanks 224

GOIN' DOWN DE MONT: A PEOPLE'S HISTORY

De Mont noticeboard 1978

GOIN' DOWN DE MONT: A PEOPLE'S HISTORY

FOREWORD

This book is a love letter. Not to a person, but to a place, or to be precise, a building – the De Montfort Hall, more affectionately known by the residents of Leicester as the De Mont.

My first introduction to the Hall was over the Christmas holiday of 1968/69. In that time-honoured British tradition, Mum and Dad took me and my brother to a panto, *Aladdin*, with Tommy Trinder, an old music hall comedian ('You lucky people!'), starring as Abanazar.

At the time, I was probably too busy yelling, 'Look behind you!' and, 'Oh, no it isn't!' to really notice my surroundings. But a year or two later, I was lucky enough to grace the De Mont's stage for my first and only time, playing xylophone for the Leicestershire Schools Orchestra or some similar-sounding outfit. It was then, looking out over the audience, that I first began to fully appreciate the beauty of the Hall. I also developed my first crush at the time on a recorder player whose name, I vaguely recall, was Tina.

I was also fortunate enough to attend classical concerts there by the Hallé Orchestra, the De Mont's resident orchestra at the time. Through the school, we got discounted tickets, and I remember sitting in the choir stalls, just in front of the giant organ pipes and behind the percussion section, feeling the bass notes vibrate in my diaphragm and watching the conductor gyrate and grimace. Looking out over the audience once more, I remember thinking that music could not have found a better home than the De Mont.

As these pages will show, I don't think I was wrong, then or now.

Then, on 2 April 1973, those thoughts took on a whole new meaning. On that night, I attended my first ever rock show at the De Mont, and Status Quo changed my life forever. From that moment, for the next decade, I saved up my pocket money, Christmas money and money from my paper round to attend as many shows as I possibly could.

In 2015, fearing that my own memories of so many incredible musical nights were starting to fade, I decided to start writing them down. For fun, I invited a group of friends who had attended many of the shows with me to write theirs down too. The result was a series of blog posts that I published to my website, brucepegg.com.

Fast forward to 2022, and my old friend Richard Houghton invited me to reach out to others who had attended rock shows at the De Mont at time and turn their stories and the blog posts into a book. I immediately agreed, and you are holding the results in your hand: a love letter to the De Mont from hundreds of people whose lives were touched by some of the greatest bands of the rock era who performed on its stage.

GOIN' DOWN DE MONT: A PEOPLE'S HISTORY

INTRODUCTION

A wide-eyed teenage boy stands precariously on a chair in the middle of a seething crowd of people. They, and he, are mesmerised by the sight of a thin, androgynous, red-haired figure in a flamboyant costume and women's makeup, singing and acting on the stage just a short distance away.

It is 11 June 1973. The larger-than-life character that has the boy and the crowd in rapt attention is David Bowie. For the boy witnessing the event from the hot, sweaty stalls of the De Montfort Hall in Leicester, the experience of this spectacle will become life changing, though he has yet to understand that. But right now, he is engrossed by it all, completely overtaken by the moment.

How do I know? Because I was that 13-year-old boy, and that moment is still etched in my mind some fifty years later. It planted the seeds of a lifelong love of music – appreciating it, performing it, writing about it.

Almost sixty years before this night, the Hall had first opened its doors, a gift to enrich the lives of the city's inhabitants, a symbol of the city's importance in Britain and its then Empire. But even the most clairvoyant of the city of Leicester's founding fathers could not have foreseen this strange event as it unfolded inside the elegant white building they had envisioned all those years ago. What moral outrage would they have expressed as a cross-dressing singer cavorted suggestively on stage, sang of sex and drugs and simulated an obscene act with his guitar player? How, might they have wondered, did we get from their world of Victorian gentility and prudishness to what must have seemed to them like a modern version of a Roman orgy?

The boy, of course, couldn't have cared less at the time, just like those in the audience around him, and many more audiences that came before and after to witness such spectacles.

These are the stories we are about to hear.

'A Town Hall capable to meet the city's needs'
Stories about the De Mont actually begin before it was even built – in 1907 to be exact. In that year, the British Association, a group dedicated to the advancement of science, came to Leicester with an eye to holding

their 77th annual meeting in the city. At the time, they came to the realisation 'that Leicester possesses no public building large enough for the purposes of holding the usual conversazione [scientific discussion] and reception of the large number of members and guests anticipated.'[1] (Well, there was The Temperance Hall on Granby Street. But it was… well… a *temperance* hall.)

They decided on a temporary solution to the problem and built a loggia – a covered, four-sided, outdoor corridor similar to a cloister – in Museum Square, off the back of the New Walk Museum, where the meetings were to be held. This wooden structure was disassembled after the meeting, though some in the city floated the idea that the whole thing should be taken up to Victoria Park and rebuilt.[2]

Clearly, taking down some wooden planks, moving them a few hundred yards to the top end of New Walk, and reassembling them was not going to be a permanent answer to the city's venue problem. Leicester needed something more substantial, but there was some debate over what final form it should take. All agreed Leicester needed 'a Town Hall capable to meet the city's needs in the matter of great meetings, concerts, lectures and entertainments', according to local historian Robert Guy Waddington. But the building that we now know as the De Mont 'was built with the intention of tiding the city over some twenty years' until the final version could be built.[3]

All of this may have led to a long-standing Leicester rumour – one that I heard from my Dad when I was a kid and have heard repeated by others since – that the Hall itself was originally designed as a temporary building. Fortunately, for those of us who came later, the solution was permanent enough to remain standing to this day, its well-proportioned gabled roof, gleaming white façade and portico with its supporting Doric columns soon becoming one of Leicester's iconic landmarks and the city's beating cultural heart for over a hundred years.

Built at a cost of £21,000[4] (a little under £3 million in 2022 currency) by the local architectural firm of Stockdale Harrison and Sons (who also built Edinburgh's famed Usher Hall in 1914), the De Montfort Hall opened on 21 July 1913. Less than a year later, on 19 February 1914, the hall's enormous pipe organ, made by local builders Stephen Taylor and Sons, was presented as a gift to the city from Alfred Corah[5], the wealthy

Leicester industrialist and owner of N. Corah and Sons, by then the largest knitwear company in Europe.

Immediately, the De Mont took its place among the other grand regional civic venues of the day: the Birmingham Town Hall (opened 1834), the Free Trade Hall in Manchester (1856), Bristol's then-named Colston Hall (1867), and later the Newcastle (1927) and Sheffield (1932) City Halls. Such venues were originally designed to be community spaces, featuring performances by local chorales, orchestras, and dramatic societies alongside national touring acts of all kinds, political events, and even boxing and wrestling bouts. Little did any of the communities they were built in realise that they would eventually play significant roles in the development of a musical genre that would become ubiquitous the world over.

'There are only three halls in Britain worth singing in'

In one important way, however, the De Mont stood apart from the other town and city halls. Shortly after it opened, Italian superstar soprano Luisa Tetrazzini uttered the oft-quoted words that, 'There are only three halls in Britain worth singing in. One in Glasgow, the Usher Hall in Edinburgh, and this one.'[5] It's a claim the Hall itself plays up in its own publicity; as I write, these words, 'De Montfort Hall's excellent reputation as a venue has been further enhanced by its acoustics, which can stand shoulder to shoulder with the best concert halls in the world,' appear on the history page of the Hall's website.[6]

Almost all of those whose words appear in this book grew up believing this to be true and would heartily agree with the sentiment. Such grandiose claims are hard to prove, of course, and can more easily be chalked up to civic pride than hard facts. But compelling evidence does exist to give the assertion some credence.

First, there is the Hall's shape, which is rectangular rather than circular or octagonal, producing clean lines that enable the sound to pass unimpeded from the stage to the back of the Hall. According to a contemporary analysis of Harrison's design by the Leicestershire Architectural and Archaeological Society, not only did this shape reduce the original construction costs, as it eliminated 'the large spans required entailing complicated and costly roofs', but 'from an acoustic point of view' the 'rectangular plan… divided into eleven bays of 14 ft. spans… has been found to be most satisfactory,' and the 'acoustic properties… have already been tested and found excellent'.[7]

Next, there is the Hall's barrel-vaulted ceiling, which further focuses and projects the sound. And last, Leicester historian John Banner has even speculated the brick piers on which the Hall was built (due to the soft ground around Victoria Park being unable to support regular foundations) also 'might account for its wonderful acoustics'.[8]

Then there is also the testimony provided by some of the musicians who have graced the Hall's stage. Steve Hackett, who has performed at the Hall many times with his own band and as the guitarist for Genesis in the Seventies, told me that the Hall is, 'One of those venues that has a unique sound. It has a particular natural reverb and ambience. It flattered the quasi-classical sound of Genesis at that time.'[9]

Leicester-born Dave Bartram, who found fame with local rock and roll revivalists Showaddywaddy in the Seventies, echoed those sentiments when he told me, 'Acoustically, the venue was quite unique in that rock artists, acoustic performers and large orchestras felt equally at home. The sound reverberated unwaveringly through every nook and cranny with very little slap-back booming from its walls, unlike many traditional high-ceilinged civic halls and cavernous exhibition centres. This makes the venue – unbiasedly – one of the more pleasurable on the theatre circuit to play.'[10]

But Cream's tour manager, Bob Adcock, who worked the Hall with Blackmore's Rainbow, Iron Maiden and Scorpions, remembers the Hall not for its sound but for its crowd. 'I don't remember the sound as being either good or bad. It wasn't the kind of place where you went, "That was fantastic," and it also wasn't the kind of place where you went, "Oh Christ, no, you won't get a good sound here." It was middle of the road as far as the sound went. It was the audience that made it.

'It was always a great atmosphere – it was always a great city for rock and roll. There was never any aggravation there; it was always easy to load in and load out, the atmosphere was always fabulous, and you were assured of a good gig when you went to De Montfort Hall. It was very much a gig you looked forward to rather than one you wanted to avoid.'[11]

In the final analysis, it's impossible to say whether it's the Hall's acoustics or its ambience that has endeared it to audiences down through the years. But most – and especially those who have told their stories here – will agree with Steve Hackett, who believes the De Mont is simply 'good for rock bands because there's a magic in the air'.[9]

A microcosm of rock music history

Regardless of the Hall's claim to acoustic perfection, the importance of the Hall in the history of rock music in the UK is not in dispute, and in the stories that follow, you can see that history unfold.

Of course, there must have been plenty of musical stories coming out of the De Mont before the rock and roll era, though few from that time remain today. Sure, all the greats appeared there: Judy Garland, Frank Sinatra, Louis Armstrong, Nat King Cole. There was even a legendary secret show by the Glenn Miller Orchestra on 11 September 1944, a morale booster for the paratroopers of the US 82nd Airborne, who had been stationed in and around Leicester and were about to be deployed in the Allies' military operation, Operation Market Garden, six days later.

For the most part, though, the Hall's calendar was dominated by classical music, performed most often between the wars by the Leicester Symphony Orchestra conducted by the legendary Sir Malcolm Sargent and, after the Second World War, by all the great British touring orchestras, including the Hallé Orchestra, the London Philharmonic and the Royal Philharmonic, conducted by Sargent and those other giants of the field, Sir John Barbirolli and Sir Thomas Beecham. It's hard to imagine stories of backstage bacchanals, crowd riots and felonious show entries coming from such refined entertainments.

No. The real stories begin some forty years after the hall opened, shortly after August 1955, when a movie, *Blackboard Jungle*, brought a new American teen music phenomenon to the British Isles. The movie included Bill Haley's anthem 'Rock Around the Clock' as part of its soundtrack; with its release, the rock and roll era in Britain arguably began.

At the time, live music venues in Britain consisted of dance halls, music clubs specialising mostly in folk and jazz, variety theatres, cinemas, and the multipurpose town and city halls.[12] And it was in the city and town halls and the Gaumont/Granada/Odeon cinema chain that Britain got its first taste of rock and roll.

But the De Mont saw precious few of the American originators though, to be fair, neither did most of the rest of Britain. Elvis Presley famously never played outside of the US in his whole career. Little Richard first toured the UK in 1962, playing mostly the cinema circuit, and never played Leicester. Chuck Berry wouldn't make it to town until 1964, when he toured on a bill with rockabilly legend Carl Perkins, while Bo Diddley made it far later, playing his lone De Mont show in 1985. And Jerry Lee Lewis was a famous no-show when his extensive 27-date tour of the UK in 1958 was cancelled after only three dates when the British press got wind that he had married his 13-year-old cousin before even divorcing his second wife. The tour, including a De Mont date on 16 June 1958, went on as scheduled without him but with American jump blues group The Treniers headlining. (Lewis eventually did make it to town in 1962.)

Of the US acts that did make it across the pond in the Fifties, the Bill Haley tour (9 February-10 March 1957) skipped the De Mont and all the other town halls, sticking to the Gaumont/Granada/Odeon cinemas due to Haley's association with the organisation that had originally released the movie *Rock Around the Clock*. But in that same period, the De Mont did host other American rock, doo wop and R&B acts.

Typically for the day, some acts were viewed as novelties: the American doo-wop, rhythm and blues and rock and roll singer Frankie Lymon, for example, headlined the De Mont on 16 May 1957, sharing a bill with an eclectic and solidly British line-up that included Terry Lightfoot and His Jazzmen, the Chas McDevitt Skiffle Group, and Scottish pop singer Billie Anthony. Buddy Holly, too, headlined on 16 March 1958, in a show that so inspired singer and guitarist Ian Hunter and Leicester's own keyboardist Jon Lord that both went on to their own illustrious careers in rock and roll a decade later.

While rock and roll made inroads into the British collective consciousness, another group of pop musicians were also garnering attention in both the US and the UK – the so-called teen idols. With their squeaky-clean looks and carefully groomed images, they represented the more acceptable face of rock and roll. Pat Boone, who visited the Hall on 3 January 1957, was a classic example. A conservative Christian, he made his reputation with sanitised versions of Fats Domino's 'Ain't That a Shame' and Little Richard's 'Tutti Frutti' and 'Long Tall Sally', which were all aimed at a more respectable young, middle-class audience.

The rise of singers like Boone and Paul Anka, who also played the Hall, was to prove the perfect vehicle for Britain to make its entry into the rock world in its own right, and in short succession, acts like Tommy Steele, Marty Wilde, Cliff Richard, Adam Faith and Billy Fury were catapulted into stardom. All played the De Mont at that time, and rock and roll began to be a fixture at the Hall and elsewhere around the country.

Still, American rockers such as Dion, Del Shannon, Eddie Cochran and Gene Vincent (who appeared at the Hall with Cochran just a month before the car crash in 1960 that took his life and almost took Cochran's) dominated the rock music scene into the early sixties, and all of them took turns on De Mont bills with homegrown British talent.

But all that was about to change. On 31 March 1963, the Hall bore witness to the early stages of arguably the most important UK rock revolution of all. Midway down a bill headlined by Americans – rocker Chris Montez and pop singer Tommy Roe – The Beatles, then a relatively unknown band from Liverpool, made their Leicester debut and upstaged their American rivals as they had done up and down the country. The Mersey Sound began to sweep the nation, and music around the world was about to be changed forever.

It was at this point that rock music exploded around Britain, and the list of performers at the De Mont from this point on reads like a rock music history book: The Beatles, the Rolling Stones, the Kinks and The Who, and American acts such as Bob Dylan and Jimi Hendrix, all played the De Mont at that time, the latter on one of the strangest bills to hit Leicester, appearing alongside American pop act the Walker Brothers, English folk singer Cat Stevens, and Leicester's own crooner Engelbert Humperdinck on 16 April 1967.

The usual practice of the day for many of the early rock and roll shows, based on the old music hall model, was for numerous acts to play two shows a day at each venue. The acts would either appear twice at each show in billing order before and after an intermission, or appear in billing order with the headlining act playing a longer set in the second half of each show. At every show, the audiences would scream so loudly that the performers, singing through the Hall's primitive PA system, were inaudible. Audience stories of the phenomenon are well-documented in these pages and elsewhere.

But around 1969, as rock finally became the dominant force in popular music, most headliners appeared on bills alone with just one or two supporting acts at most. And so began what was arguably the greatest decade in rock music's, and the De Mont's, history. A quick glance over the shows played at the Hall in the Seventies reveals a 'who's who' of rock royalty: Led Zeppelin, Deep Purple, ELP, Eric Clapton, T.Rex, Black Sabbath, Status Quo, David Bowie, Santana, Lynyrd Skynyrd, Rush, AC/DC, the Clash – the list goes on. In fact, it would probably be easier to name the acts that didn't play there during that time.

As it has done throughout its history, the Hall continued to be a microcosm of the music world, hosting acts of each successive musical wave that washed across the country. At the height of glam rock, for example, in June of 1973, you could have seen David Bowie, Sweet, Wizzard and Gary Glitter all within a fortnight.

Earlier that year, too, the cheers of a De Mont audience were recorded and later heard on the album *Genesis Live*, the first of many recordings made at the Hall that were legitimately released. (Lord only knows how many bootlegs came out of the place.) That album, in part, also helped to boost the De Mont's boast of having superior acoustics.

Later that decade, the Clash (28 May 1977) and the Damned (28 November 1977) headlined the first punk shows at the Hall, while several bills in 1979 and early 1980 – Motörhead with Girlschool on 8 April 1979, AC/DC with Def Leppard on 9 November 1979, Motörhead again, this time with Saxon on 14 November 1979, and Judas Priest with Iron Maiden on 13 March 1980 – saw the birth of the so-called New Wave of British Heavy Metal. And appearances by the Police on 9 September 1979, just days before 'Message in a Bottle' hit number 1 and placed them on the cusp of worldwide stardom, and an unsigned and completely unknown Duran Duran supporting new wave singer Hazel O'Connor on 2 December 1980, also pointed the way to the musically diverse decade that lay ahead.

All the while, stage shows continued to evolve into the kinds of performances we know and expect today. Bands started bringing their own bigger, more technologically sophisticated (and much louder) PA systems, while bands like Rainbow, Rush, and Genesis pioneered increasingly more elaborate light shows.

Decline and rebirth

It was at this point my own association with the Hall sadly ended when I emigrated to the United States in 1981. But the De Mont continued to see its share of 'you shoulda been there' shows: U2 on 3 December 1982, the third date of their *Pre-War* tour that started in small European halls and ended in massive US arenas, Frankie Goes to Hollywood on 15 March 1985 during the height of their brief but spectacular year-long siege on British music and culture, and INXS on 8 February 1988, just a few months after the release of *Kick* and at the height of their game, are just a few examples.

By the end of the Eighties, however, the De Mont began to see fewer and fewer rock acts. There are a number of reasons for that – some social, some factual, some conjecture. First, there was the general decline of rock music as a cultural force. The increasing popularity of other, non-guitar-based music, and a greater number of recreation options, such as satellite and cable television and the internet, meant that rock no longer enjoyed the influential place in the entertainment landscape it had previously occupied.

Then there was the increasing competition posed by the opening of both comparable and larger venues close to Leicester, such as the National Exhibition Centre (NEC) (opened 1976) and Arena Birmingham (1991) in Birmingham, Rock City (1980) and Motorpoint Arena (2000) in Nottingham, and Sheffield Arena (1991). Touring acts had more choices of Midlands venues than ever, and the De Mont could no longer rely on rock bands being frequent visitors anymore.

The Hall, too, changed significantly in the Nineties with the installation of a downstairs seating system in 1994. This enabled the stalls to be reconfigured in several different ways, including general admission without seats, floor seating and tiered seating. In some ways, the renovation marked a return to the Hall's original multipurpose remit, allowing it to stage more intimate and varied performances.

Around this time, rumours began circulating of the City Council enacting a rock music booking ban, or at least a non-cooperation policy with rock music promoters, at the De Mont. Like the Hall's legendary acoustic superiority, these things are hard to prove or refute, but at least one local promoter and musician, Nick Murphy, was quoted in 1999 as saying, 'The De Montfort Hall is impossible to book. I've looked at stuff before and said, "Let's put that on at De Montfort Hall." But their stumbling blocks before you have started are so massive, their criteria for who they want to have on are a fucking joke… The venue is supposed to have one of the best sounds in the country. Bands and orchestras alike say it has the best acoustics in the country, yet you can't get it.'[13]

But the Hall, as any savvy venue does, moved with the times and entered the millennium continuing to cater to the demands of its patrons, including rock audiences, albeit in a different way. Fuelled by nostalgia, baby boomers opened up a market for legacy acts, mostly from the Sixties but with few original musicians and, in some cases, just one founding member and dubious claims to the band's name. But that didn't stop people flocking to package tours such as *Sixties Gold* and *Sensational 60s*, reminiscent of the Fifties and Sixties tours that got the ball rolling in the first place.

And if the real thing was not available, punters started to shell out good money for tribute acts such as The Bootleg Beatles, The Australian Pink Floyd Show and Brit Floyd, assorted Queen tribute bands, and The Musical Box, an authentic portrayal of Seventies-era Genesis. Such shows have dominated the De Mont's calendar in recent years, though rock concerts at the venue continue on with shows by touring rock stalwarts such as Marillion, and Leicester's own up-and-comers Kasabian, who made their Hall debut in 2006.

Here, then, is one chapter of the De Mont story – its rock music legacy – presented in the words and pictures of those whose lives were changed, sometimes in small ways and sometimes in large, as happened to the boy at the David Bowie show, by their experiences *Goin' Down De Mont*.

GOIN' DOWN DE MONT: A PEOPLE'S HISTORY

Sources

[1] The Leicester Meeting of the British Association. *Nature* 75, 585 (1907). https://www.nature.com/articles/075585a0.pdf

[2] Goddard, Jane. 'Vintage photo showcases "remarkable edifice" built in heart of Edwardian Leicester'. *Leicester Mercury*, 16 Jul. 2019. https://www.leicestermercury.co.uk/news/history/vintage-photo-showcases-remarkable-edifice-3096061.

[3] Waddington, Robert Guy. *Leicester: The Making of a Modern City*. Gibbons, Leicester: 1931.

[4] http://www.arthurlloyd.co.uk/LeicesterTheatres/DemontfortHallLeicester.htm

[5] https://www.storyofleicester.info/leisure-entertainment/de-montfort-hall/

[6] https://www.demontforthall.co.uk/history/

[7] *Transactions of the Leicestershire Architectural and Archaelogical Society*, Volume XI, 1913-1914.

[8] Banner, John. *Out and About in Leicester: A Series of Armchair Tours*. Leicester City Council Living History Unit, Leicester: 1994.

[9] Steve Hackett. Personal email to the author. 21 October 2021.

[10] Dave Bartram. Personal email to the author. 2 November 2021.

[11] Bob Adcock. Interview with Richard Houghton. 28 July 2022.

[12] Frith, Simon; Matt Brennan, Martin Cloonan, and Emma Webster. *The History of Live Music in Britain, Vol. 1: 1950-1967*. Routledge: Abingdon, Oxon. 2016.

[13] Gilmore, Abigail. *Popular music in the city: an examination of local music scenes, popular music practice and cultural policy in the city of Leicester*. University of Leicester Doctoral Thesis, 1999. https://leicester.figshare.com/articles/thesis/Popular_music_in_the_city_an_examination_of_local_music_scenes_popular_music_practice_and_cultural_policy_in_the_city_of_Leicester/10179566/1

GOIN' DOWN DE MONT: A PEOPLE'S HISTORY

GOIN' DOWN DE MONT: A PEOPLE'S HISTORY

BUDDY HOLLY
16 MARCH 1958

IAN HUNTER, MOTT THE HOOPLE

I was about 15 or 16 when [rock and roll] hit. I wasn't good enough to participate until eight, ten or twelve years later, but as a fan I was into everything from the age of fifteen. We lived in Northampton and there was a band in town called The Homelanders who were three blond-headed kids. Their father had a dry-cleaning business, and they said they were going to see this bloke at Leicester De Montfort on the bus, so off we went and saw Buddy Holly. It was the first time I had ever seen Strat guitars and he had six of them. People were rushing to the stage and kissing his feet and I thought, 'Well, yeah, he's good but I ain't going down there!' You never heard the double bass or the snare; they were just all round one low-resolution mic. He had an amp that was taller than him – it was probably a 20W or something – and these six Strats which were all different colours. It was like something from outer space because all we had in England were Hofners.

(as told to Glenn Williams)

JON LORD, DEEP PURPLE

This place where I am standing now [the De Montfort Hall] is pretty much seminal in my life. I came to my first concert here at the age of, I think, six or seven years old. My parents brought me to see the Hallé Orchestra with the saintly Sir John Barberolli

Jon Lord (Deep Purple/Whitesnake) on stage at the De Montfort Hall receiving an Honorary Degree in Music from the University of Leicester, 26 July 2011. Inset: Jon Lord on stage at the De Montfort Hall with Whitesnake, 2 June 1980

conducting. I actually remember the programme – it was cutting edge classical stuff: the 'William Tell Overture', Grieg's *Piano Concerto* and the *New World Symphony*… It thrilled me and, I think, possibly changed things right then and there. In this same hall, as a teenager, I saw Buddy Holly, which spun my head around. And I think the love of what Buddy Holly represented and the love of what the Hallé Orchestra represented has defined my musical life.

(after receiving an Honorary Degree of Doctor of Music from the University of Leicester, 26 July 2011)

EDDIE COCHRAN & GENE VINCENT
18 FEBRUARY 1960

MARILYN GREEN
This was just before The Beatles came on the scene, so there were no teenagers screaming, just fans clapping and tapping their feet. Gene Vincent was top of the bill. I can't remember who else was on the show. I was only bothered about Eddie Cochran and he came on first but he also joined Gene at the end. It was a fantastic night. I was 15 and I adored Eddie. It broke my heart when he died just after that.

BOBBY DARIN, DUANE EDDY & THE REBELS, CLYDE MCPHATTER
20 MARCH 1960

JOHN STRETTON
My first introduction to the wonderful De Montfort Hall in Leicester was in my last full year at Loughborough College School, when I went with two classmates to a concert of classical music, including what would become my favourite piece of the genre, Beethoven's *Third Symphony* ('The Eroica').

It was not long, however, before my rock life at the venue began, when I went, accompanied by my parents, to see Bobby Darin, Clyde McPhatter and Duane Eddy. Despite 'Dream Lover' being one of my favourite pop songs at the time, my main interest was to see Duane and The Rebels after hearing his music on the radio (Radio Luxembourg, I think).

The evening was an unmitigated delight, including an appreciation of Clyde McPhatter (who I had never heard before) and ending with a meeting with Duane at the stage door after the show. Over subsequent years I met and became friends with Duane, and I reminded him of this first meeting exactly 60 years later, in 2020.

CLIFF RICHARD
24 SEPTEMBER 1961

JACKIE SIMON
I saw loads of concerts at the De Mont. The ones I remember most, being a big fan of his, are the Cliff Richard shows. I used to go with my friend Linda. We would go to the matinee straight from her house after changing after school. My dad was very strict. He always knew what time the buses were, and he knew more or less exactly what time I was due home. Everything always went well until one concert, when we stood outside the dressing rooms with the crowd shouting for Cliff. Needless to say, I missed my first bus, which had a knock-on effect on the next bus which would take me home. When I got off the bus there was my dad waiting. He was not happy. He said, 'That's it. You are not going again!'

THE CLIFF RICHARD SHOW WITH THE SHADOWS
8 MARCH 1962

PAMELA BLENCO
Before the birth of rock 'n' roll, I saw the American singer Guy Mitchell twice at the De Montfort Hall. I went with my friend from school, Marion, on the train. We just walked up from the station. We were 13. We'd try and see him when we could. There used to be a ticket agency in Rushden in Northamptonshire, where I lived, called Neville's where

you could buy tickets but sometimes we sent off for tickets by post. The *New Musical Express* would advertise the concerts. We wanted to go and see Johnny Ray there as well but we couldn't get in so we went to the London Palladium to see him.

And we saw Ella Fitzgerald in March 1961. She appeared with the Oscar Peterson Trio. There were two shows scheduled and I was going to go just with my sister. But the early evening performance was cancelled because there wasn't enough demand for tickets and they wrote to us and changed our tickets. We wouldn't have been able to get home from the late evening performance on public transport so I had to ask my brother if he wanted to come and he took us to the show in his Morris Traveller. Everybody was shouting for Ella to sing 'Manhattan' and she reckoned she didn't know it. But she said she'd have a go and did a bit of scat singing in the middle, so she really didn't know it!

I went to see Cliff Richard with my niece, Rosemary, because she liked Cliff. The Shadows did the opening set and quite a few things of their own things, and it was only when I saw them at this show that I appreciated what they've done. After the interval, they came out backing Cliff. Cliff and The Shadows did some comedy stuff between the songs, so it was almost like pantomime. Cliff would do a similar thing on his TV show.

An album recorded on that tour at the ABC Theatre in Kingston, Surrey and later released by EMI would suggest that The Shadows opened with 'Apache' and played a set that included 'Wonderful Land' and 'FBI'. Cliff started his 12 song set with 'Do You Wanna Dance' and concluded with a three song medley including 'The Young Ones' and 'We Say Yeah'.

JERRY LEE LEWIS, JOHNNY KIDD & THE PIRATES
30 APRIL 1962

ROGER CHAPMAN, FAMILY
I performed at the De Mont with Family and Streetwalkers, but my most memorable times were seeing other artists – Gene Vincent, Muddy Waters, the Stones, Dusty Springfield, Peter Gabriel and lots of others.

My best memory is of seeing Jerry Lee Lewis not long after he was deported for having an underage wife. This was not illegal in the US but illegal in the UK, apparently. At the end of Jerry's show, I jumped on the stage, ran through the stage left door (I only know that after gigging there myself a few times), and he was standing there, so of course I asked for his autograph. He graciously signed my entrance ticket stub before the bouncers got me. I often think about this and wish I still had the ticket stub he signed.

JOHN STRETTON
Cousin Dave accompanied me on this occasion, and we both thoroughly enjoyed the whole show but wanted more. At the end we dashed backstage, with the intent of meeting Jerry Lee. No one would tell us which dressing room he was in until Johnny Kidd (by this time without his eye patch!) took pity on us and indicated a door we might try. We knocked, and voice said 'Come in.' We did, and there was the great man, totally on his own.

He beckoned us in. This was shortly after his child had died in a swimming pool, so we were careful on what we asked/spoke about, but he was charming, courteous and prepared to discuss his emotions. We spent roughly fifteen minutes with him, and then shook his hand and left him. There was no sign of the cantankerous 'Killer' that so many report.

CHRIS MONTEZ, TOMMY ROE, THE BEATLES, VISCOUNTS, TERRY YOUNG SIX & DEBBIE LEE: COMPERE TONY MARSH
31 MARCH 1963

GERALDINE HOPES (NÉE BEADLE)
This was my very first concert when I was 13. It was a concert that I can remember to this day. I adored Chris Montez's and Tommy Roe's songs, but I fell in love with the music of the support band on the tour – The Beatles! The seats were simply wooden chairs all on the same level, and if one was

in the seats furthest away from the stage, one had to stand to get any sight of the stage whatsoever. So, with De Mont having sold around 50 to 60 per cent of their tickets, and the expensive seats nearer the stage being only half full, they were soon filled by the audience from the cheap seats.

It was an amazing concert and probably only one of a few Beatles concerts attended by so few people. By the time of The Beatles' second concert at the De Mont, in December 1963, I was unable to get a ticket – people had camped out at the Town Hall box office overnight, and all tickets had been sold. Disappointed as I was, I felt that I'd had the privilege of seeing them before they became famous, and it is one of my favourite memories.

ALAN DUTTON

We started to queue at around 10pm. I was with my then girlfriend, who later became my wife, and one of her friends was with us. The ticket office was in the council offices on Charles Street, but the queue was already around to the back of Lewis's in Fox Lane. At around 3am, the police decided to consolidate the queue and moved everybody up. What was a fairly orderly crowd suddenly became a mad dash and then an almighty crush. We finished up outside Halfords – the crush was that bad I heard a cracking, and the shop window went in. Fortunately no one was hurt.

The show itself was amazing. The noise from the audience was horrific, but the atmosphere was like nothing I have experienced before or even after. A memory to last a lifetime. I also remember Tommy Roe and Chris Montez on the bill and an American girl group, the name of which I can't remember.

GLENISE LEE

I have forgotten the boyfriend(s) who paid for the tickets, but I do remember three evenings spent at the city's De Montfort Hall. I went with a boy on 23 March 1963 to see Cliff Richard. The hall was full. Sold out. The girls were screaming. The following week, 31 March 1963, we went to see The Beatles. The hall was not full. Tickets were still available. There was some screaming.

It's because of the lower noise level, when the boys on stage could make themselves and their songs heard, that I remember hearing a heckler. After one song, after the applause and screaming had subsided to the level that my dad would have called 'still far too loud for comfort', a heckler from the audience shouted something that John Lennon didn't like. John crossed to the front of the stage, glared down at the audience and said, 'The last time I saw a mouth that big, it had a hook in it!'

My boyfriend struggled to get tickets for The Beatles' concert on 1 December 1963. We had to fight through crowds of shrieking fans to get into the concert. We were near to the coach that was delivering the band. Later, I realised I'd lost a button from my winter coat in the scrum. Screaming? The roof was lifted! After the concert, I found my button. Metal, the size of a half crown, it had been flattened by the coach. I treasured that button for years.

BILLY FURY & CILLA BLACK
10 NOVEMBER 1963

BRIAN HOLLAND

I went to see Billy Fury, and there was a red-headed girl sitting in front of us with a blond-haired guy. After the interval, first up was the girl sitting in front of us. It was Cilla Black, and she said it was her first big public appearance. She said she was friends with The Beatles, and the first song she sang was by 'Love of the Loved' by John and Paul. I had never heard of her before that night but always liked her after that performance.

DUANE EDDY, THE SHIRELLES, GENE VINCENT & GARY US BONDS
24 NOVEMBER 1963

JOHN STRETTON

In the company of my new girlfriend Denise, I was in the stalls for the first (5.40pm) performance. Needless to say, I was pleased to introduce Denise to the music of Duane Eddy and we both again thoroughly enjoyed the entertainment, although a dispute over work permits meant the Rebels could not back Duane for much of the tour. He was backed by the Flintstones at De Mont.

As we were about to leave the theatre, we overheard a conversation that seemed to indicate some of the artists were proposing to adjourn to a local pub in nearby London Road. We went there as well, hoping perhaps to meet Duane. We were unlucky on that count, but we did join the Shirelles' party in the bar and listened to their off-duty banter. Once more, all very polite and human without any star trappings.

Having learned that we did not have tickets for the second show, they said we should 'mention their names' at the Hall and we would be allowed in… and it worked! We found two empty seats and enjoyed the treat a second time. The initial 8/6 ticket price had proved mighty fine value!

THE BEATLES
1 DECEMBER 1963

PAM CHRITCHLOW

My friend Gloria and I chatted to a couple of guys after the show. They were with two limousines. The bloke I chatted to invited us to the Beatles aftershow party, which was taking place in a house in Knighton. Unfortunately, I didn't believe him. After he had driven off, Gloria asked what we'd talked about. She went mad when I told her as she knew he was Brian Epstein! I just thought he seemed very different to anyone I had ever met before.

Ticket queue in October 1963 at Charles Street Municipal Box Office for The Beatles 1 December 1963 performance

Photos – John Langham

STUART LANGFORD

I used to go to school at the Wyggeston Boys just up University Road from the De Mont, and I walked to school the day after The Beatles had played. I didn't go and see them – I didn't really know how important they were – but the pavement outside was completely covered in a kind of squidgy mess of pressed-in Jelly Babies. One of The Beatles had foolishly said Jelly Babies were their favourite sweet in one of those daft questions they get asked, so fans were flinging boxes and packets and quarter pounds of Jelly Babies at them wherever they played. The whole pavement outside the next morning after was a kind of gooey, sticky, multi-coloured mess of trodden-in Jelly Babies. And I remember walking past with my mate that morning and saying, 'What the hell's happened here?'

ANN STEVEN

I think it was just before they released 'I Wanna Hold Your Hand'. I was in row M on my own. I had paid £1/10s for the ticket off a friend at school. I tried to get to the front but security took me back to my seat. Then a lad jumped off the balcony and onto the stage.

THE ROLLING STONES
26 JANUARY 1964

WENDY FROST

The Hall was packed solid and all the teenagers were shouting and singing Stones songs. The place was buzzing with excitement. I was there with my boyfriend and we were both wet with sweat at the thought of the Stones music. The curtains opened and the crowd went wild, screaming. The band looked great and Brian Jones, the leader, always looked very smart and well groomed. When the show finished my boyfriend and I left there in a hypnotic haze and walked down London Road where all the other Stones fans were talking and singing and very happy. A Stones fan for life!

GOIN' DOWN DE MONT: A PEOPLE'S HISTORY

MARTIN OSBORN

We saw the Stones a number of times, mostly at the De Montfort Hall in Leicester where they appeared with, amongst others, Phil Spector's very sexy girl group the Ronettes, Joe Brown and the Bruvvers and the Spencer Davis Group. We stopped going to see them because we could not hear the band over the screaming girls.

GISELA OAKES

A friend called Penny Williams and I bought tickets for the concert at the De Montfort Hall because we were great fans of the Rolling Stones. We were both nearly 16 and had chosen our clothes very carefully. In those days, most teenagers were either Mods or Rockers, and we considered ourselves as Dolly Rocker Mods. I'd bought some bright green pumps with tartan on them, so I made a bright green dress with tartan bib and collar to match and one of those funny caps that were in vogue then.

We travelled to Leicester from Northampton by coach. I can't remember much about the actual performance, but by this time we'd struck up conversation with a boy, older than us, who wasn't a roadie but who seemed to know the Rolling Stones slightly. After the concert was over, he beckoned for us to follow him up the right hand side of the stage. All I can remember then is Brian Jones and Mick Jagger at a long table, clearing up. I really cannot remember what was said, only that they were both charming and friendly to us. Mick Jagger said goodbye and went off to do whatever he was doing, and Brian Jones brought photos with autographs. I can remember thinking how quiet, shy, calm and gentle he was.

By this time, we were in such a panic because we'd missed the last coach back to Northampton. In those days, people used to hitch hike a lot so we hitched a lift with a lorry driver who brought us back to Northampton. I'd missed the last red bus home, so thought I'd try the green bus at the Derngate Bus Station but that one had gone also. I got home somehow – and my parents were very relieved to see me!

THE ROLLING STONES
9 FEBRUARY 1964

DAVE BARTRAM, SHOWADDYWADDY

I was eleven years of age and have to say I went home rather disappointed as I barely heard a note thanks to the multitude of hysterical screaming teenage girls creating pandemonium in the rows ahead of me. As I recall the support band on the gig was the Paramounts featuring Gary Brooker on keys and vocals.

JULIE HEAVISIDE

I bought a cheap ticket as I was a teenager. They weren't yet very popular. My seat was near the back, but there were a lot of empty seats near the front, so my friend and I moved there. We had a brilliant view.

DAVE CLARK FIVE, THE HOLLIES, THE KINKS, MARK WYNTER, THE TREBLETONES & THE MOJOS: COMPERE FRANK BERRY
31 MARCH 1964

NICK HAIRS

The only reason I went, after a school friend suggested it, was because the Kinks were on the bill, and I was really into British R&B – the Animals, the Rolling Stones, the Graham Bond Organisation and so on. My parents were very much against it as it was a school day. I must have been a good boy!

These package tours only enabled the bands to play maybe three or four songs – usually their hits. The Kinks stole the show for me just because they played with lots of force. I seem to recall a spat between the two brothers. The Mojos were typical British R&B and I enjoyed their set. The Hollies were really professional, and their harmonies were just like the records. The Dave Clark Five just didn't press any buttons for me. I didn't like their records and I have a feeling I left before they finished their set. As for the rest of the bill, I have no memory at all.

GOIN' DOWN DE MONT: A PEOPLE'S HISTORY

CHUCK BERRY, CARL PERKINS, BRENDA LEE, THE ANIMALS, KINGSIZE TAYLOR, THE OTHER TWO & THE NASHVILLE TEENS: COMPERE LARRY BURNS
24 MAY 1964

TED GARRATT

Myself and two friends ran away from home and landed in London. We were all round 16 years of age and saw this as a life changing opportunity. The first night we spent skulking round Soho, mixing and mingling with some extremely dodgy characters. We stole bread and milk from shops and tried to sleep on park benches. On the second night we found ourselves in Wardour Street and managed to talk our way into a club called La Discotheque. We later found out this was a notorious and dangerous place to be, as it was filled with gangster types and there were drugs everywhere. Late in the evening two of us decided to leave, and when we did so, we were arrested by the police and taken to West End Central, kept overnight and put on a train home to Hinckley the next morning.

Chuck Berry 1964 UK tour programme

We were obviously the subject of a lot of attention and, during this time, I was asked by some friends if I was interested in going to the De Mont. It turned out that one of my heroes, Chuck Berry, was appearing. I had become aware of Chuck Berry because of the number of bands who cited him as an influence, in particular the Rolling Stones who had recorded 'Come On' as their first single and played more of his songs on stage.

We were all very familiar with the De Montfort Hall and loved it as a venue, so it was great to be asked to go. Also on the bill were the Swinging Blue Jeans and the Animals. Excellent as Chuck Berry was, it was the Animals who stole the evening. Their British blues was very exciting, and the use of the organ and Eric Burdon as vocalist was stunning. Chuck Berry was great but didn't particularly engage with the audience.

The evening rounded off a major week in my life and, as ever, the De Montfort Hall played a major part in it.

THE BEATLES
10 OCTOBER 1964

VALERIE PEGG

I can remember when The Beatles came to the De Montfort Hall in 1963 and how the queues were endless around the old municipal offices in Charles Street. So, when we heard that tickets were going on sale on Sunday 23 August 1964, we decided to try and get some. My sister Chris, her friend Ibby and I went to the De Montfort Hall on the day before at about teatime to join the queue around the metal fence around the Hall. There weren't too many people in the queue at that time, so we knew we would stand a good chance of getting some tickets. I stayed for a bit but, unfortunately, I wasn't allowed to queue overnight, so my dad collected me. I remember he did go back during the night to check on Chris and Ibby. My sister remembered her time in the queue as a thrilling experience; she said it was cold and she can remember having 'fun' with lads around them! The next day I was highly delighted when my sister showed me three tickets, centre stage view, three rows from the front – brilliant!

We went to the 6.15pm performance. Our seats were great, and the buzz of the crowd just got louder the more people filled the hall. The support acts came on: the Rustiks, Sounds Incorporated, the Remo Four, Tommy Quickly and Mary Wells. All were good, but the audience only wanted to see The Beatles.

When they finally came on, the non-stop screaming, standing on the chairs and mass hysteria started. I couldn't hear any of the songs that they sang and we were at the front! I did look at a playlist years later just to see what they did sing and was surprised to see it was only ten songs.

We were also surprised to see that on our row a couple of seats along from where my sister was sitting was Brian Epstein. He just sat there very quietly watching, which looked odd compared to everyone else just screaming.

They didn't appear on stage for very long and I can remember wishing I could've seen it all again.

SUE LAWRENCE

I remember seeing The Beatles at the De Mont with my friends. My Granny was a St John's nurse and used to do 'duties' there – I guess this was first aid cover. She managed to get backstage at this concert and went looking for autographs. She was given this photo with handwritten autographs on the back. However, I don't think they are genuine. They're either all done by Ringo or maybe one of the roadies or backstage staff. All I can remember is the music and the screaming. Think I and my friends were exhausted at the end of the night!

Sue Lawrence's granny got a set of fake Beatles autograph

VANESSA COX

I attended the 1964 Beatles performance at the age of 13. My friend's sister queued all night to get tickets for us. I remember it was a very cold and foggy night and my parents went with me to the De Mont. Once I'd found my friend, they left and said they would be back at the end of the show. We were so excited. We had very good seats, downstairs and only about seven rows back from the front. I seem to remember the seats and seat backs were made of canvas.

As soon as The Beatles came on stage, my friend and myself (and everyone else) stood on our seats and screamed our heads off. We could hardly hear them singing. I had worn a pair of leather gloves as it was so cold out and I had bitten the fingers and pulled them apart during the performance. I found my parents at the end and I could hardly talk, I had screamed so much. I could hardly talk the next day either. Fabulous memories!

JOHN SPENCER
I recall queuing all night for tickets to the Beatles concert in 1964. That was quite memorable, and I did manage to secure two tickets for my then girlfriend and me. Unfortunately she dumped me before the concert, so I asked that she pay the money for the ticket back to me, but she could keep the ticket I had given her. With some bad grace, she did.

On the night, I was in my seat awaiting the show to start when some girl I didn't know came and sat next to me. In doing so, she screwed her stiletto heel into my foot as she passed. I thought it was deliberate, and as she settled in her seat she asked if I was John Spencer. I denied that I was and she seemed disappointed.

The concert progressed, not that I heard much apart from the screaming girls who all went wild. I never spoke to the girl in the seat next to me, and she didn't seem to be enjoying it at all.

As an aside, I had arranged with a mate who was in the St John's Ambulance, stewarding the backstage area, to get the Beatles' autographs for me if he could. He did, and gave them to me after the show, which was kind of him. They were like gold dust and still are; I wonder what money they may be worth now?

THE ROLLING STONES
13 OCTOBER 1965

NICK HAIRS
This was another typical British pop package tour. Of course, I wanted to see the Stones, but the Spencer Davis Group really interested me and they were excellent. I think they did four songs which were their hits. The Stones were exciting, but the gig was spoilt by all the girls screaming. I had seen the Stones earlier on in the year at the Trocadero, and I thought they were better then.

KAREN SMITH

A little group of us went. A friend's dad took us. I had just been on holiday and had bought one of those great big novelty combs that you can buy at the seaside. I'd got this comb with me because it was all about their hair. The Beatles and the Stones were always being got at for their hair. I threw the comb on stage as a bit of a joke and Mick Jagger picked it up and did his hair with it!

BOB DYLAN
2 MAY 1965

TED GARRATT

Myself and a friend caught the 658 bus from Hinckley to go to the De Montfort Hall with the hope of seeing Bob Dylan – hope because we did not have tickets, so we were prepared to buy tickets or wait around and see what happened. We had become aware of Dylan through his early albums and, at that time, he was one of the few Americans, other than the legendary blues players, we were interested in.

The concert was sold out and there didn't seem to be any bootleg tickets around. We hung around outside the De Mont all through enjoying the concert, which we could hear but not see. During this time, we spoke to a number of doormen asking if they would let us in. All of them said 'no'.

At the end of the concert, we were just about to give up and head off to catch the bus home when one of the doormen said we could sneak in for the encore. We stood down the side of the Hall and took in the atmosphere. The crowd were very excited but seemed fairly restrained. Dylan was alone on the stage with, as I recall it, some of the audience seated behind him. He cut a fascinating figure with his on stage manner. From memory he did 'The Lonesome Death of Hattie Carroll', 'All I Really Want to Do' and 'It's All Over Now, Baby Blue' as the encores. I also have a clear memory of hearing 'Gates of Eden', but that was probably in the main part of the concert. Afterwards we hitchhiked back from Leicester to Hinckley.

NICK HAIRS

It was another packed house at De Mont for this concert. They even had seating behind Mr Dylan on the stage. I was on the right-hand stalls area, about 15 rows back – a good position for the view and the sound. The only noise was after each number, with rapturous applause, and sometimes, as he started a new number and the audience recognised the intro. The highlight for me was hearing him sing 'A Hard Rain's A-Gonna Fall', which is probably my favourite Bob Dylan song.

BOB DYLAN
15 MAY 1966

NICK HAIRS

A night I will never forget. I was seated in the balcony on the left of the stage, first row, so I was looking right across the front of the stage. The show was in two parts, with Dylan doing an acoustic set in the first half. After the intermission, The Band followed him on to the stage. Already you could hear the boos. Stooopid idiots! Then it all kicked off and I was in heaven.

JOHN STRETTON

The next couple of years saw the culture change from the rock and roll era into the new wave, forged by bands like The Beatles and the Rolling Stones. But for me, the next real highlight was the first appearance in Leicester by Bob Dylan. By now I had a new, regular girlfriend, Gill, and we would spend hours listening to his albums. We were happy and satisfied with the occasion, and we were back a year later for the 1966 concert.

Bob Dylan in 1966

Photo - John Stretton

Sadly, the tickets were now 15/- (75p) each, as opposed to 8/6 (42p) the year before. We joined the queue to enter the theatre and found ourselves being interviewed and filmed, asking us about our love of his music and whether we would ever boo him. We both had a definite 'no!' Apparently, the previous night (at Manchester or Liverpool, I cannot recall which) the set had been acoustic for the first half before The Band joined him onstage for a more raucous electronic half. There had been cries of anger and somewhere a cry of 'Judas!'

Not knowing what to make of all this, we were somewhat prepared for the second half onslaught, which did sound alien to what we had been expecting. But, no, we did not boo!

JOHN LEE

I went to both Dylan concerts (in '65 and '66), but at this distance I can't remember much about them beyond some of the audience booing and leaving when the (electric) second half of the 1966 concert started. Needless to say, I thought he was brilliant both times. I was an avid Dylan fan and a friend who knew the local promoter got a ticket for me for the first one. Then for the second, the De Montfort Hall gave priority booking to people who attended two concerts (of various acts) and obtained vouchers (or it may have just been the ticket stubs). These were subsequently exchanged (with cash, of course) for the 1966 tickets.

One of these concerts was for Pentangle, who I had never heard of, but they were brilliant and I've been a fan of them ever since.

SALLY WITHERS (NÉE HARRIS)

I was 16 at the time and remember the excitement about seeing him. The first half was great with his usual stuff, but the second half being electrified caused controversy. When it started the whole place was stunned – there was some jeering but as it went on most people went along with it. We were all just shocked as we didn't expect that at all! Everyone was talking about it, and I remember being disappointed as it was so far removed from his usual style. But I couldn't wait to tell my sister Yvonne all about it.

I always loved his acoustic music best but did grow to enjoy his other stuff later.

GOIN' DOWN DE MONT: A PEOPLE'S HISTORY

GEOFF TOVELL

In 1966 I was a student at the North Staffordshire College of Technology in Stoke-on-Trent. I used to return home for weekends to the family address in Coalville. I had already started to collect Dylan's albums. I vaguely remember some friends going to see Dylan at De Mont in '65. I somehow missed it but I was there the following year. It may have been my very first visit to De Montfort Hall.

Bob Dylan 1966 UK tour programme

In the first half, Dylan stood alone with just his guitar and harmonica. He sang many of the old favourites including 'Blowin' in the Wind', and I seem to remember that he ended the half with 'Desolation Row', the first time I ever heard it. In the second half, The Band came on and Dylan went electric. This received a mixed response from the audience. Some found it okay, but for many the shock was too great and they voted with their feet. Quite a lot left – I would guess at least a third of the audience.

I made a note of what he played that night. Solo, he played 'She Belongs to Me', 'Just Like a Woman', 'It's All Over Now, Baby Blue', 'Desolation Row' and 'Mr Tambourine Man'. With The Band, he played 'I Know You Know', 'I Don't Believe You', 'Baby, Let Me Follow You Down', 'Leopard-Skin Pill-Box Hat', 'One Too Many Mornings' and 'Like a Rolling Stone'.

In 2000 I was tempted to go to see Bob again at the NEC in Birmingham. I'm glad that I went but I have to say that I really preferred the first version. He did 'Blowin' in the Wind' at the NEC. I am certain of that, because I only realised what it was when it had nearly finished.

A few years ago, I went with my wife to Birmingham Symphony Hall to see the City of Birmingham Symphony Orchestra playing Schubert's *Great C Major Symphony*. Pre-concert, we went for a meal in Bank restaurant. On the next table were a bunch of younger folks who were obviously Dylan fans. They all wore Dylan t-shirts and Bob was appearing at the NIA that night. As we got up to leave, I went over to the 'youngsters', leant over their table and said, 'Have a wonderful evening gentlemen, I was there in 1966.' They stared at me in awe. It felt great that we had something in common, but that my experience went back to before they were born.

BEACH BOYS & LULU
9 NOVEMBER 1966

JOHN SPENCER

Lulu was the warmup act and was in a pretty short skirt. My mates and I were on the front row, and for one song a guy brought on a tall stool for her to sit on. Well, small girl, short skirt and tall stool led to a quite long flash of her knickers for us on the front row! I'm not sure she realised what we were cheering for.

The Beach Boys were brilliant, and I was particularly enjoying what was their new song, 'Good Vibrations', played by one on an instrument I had never seen before – a kind of horizontal stringed-neck something to make the distinctive sound. It looked like a cross between a guitar and an organ.

THE FOUR TOPS
5 FEBRUARY 1967

ANTHONY HOLT

I was able to take in my portable (it wouldn't be called that today) reel-to-reel tape recorder and recorded most of a brilliant concert from the circle. I seem to recall it wasn't too bad reproduction although sometimes spoilt by my mates (I think Neil and Ian McEwan) and I singing along.

The recorder with tape was still in my car (a Singer Gazelle) when I later went to see The Who at the Granby Halls Rag Rave. I ended up in the Leicester Royal Infirmary after somewhat foolishly, and no doubt arrogantly, saying to someone who asked if I had a light (I was smoking at the time) that 'No, I hadn't.' I never got to see The Who, as my parents had to drive the car and me back home. The car had been broken into, and my recorder with the tape in it had been taken. I forgive whoever put me in hospital, as I was obviously then a pretentious twat and probably deserved it, but not the swine who took my recorder and tape. It would be great to listen to that tape today.

GOIN' DOWN DE MONT: A PEOPLE'S HISTORY

THE WALKER BROTHERS, CAT STEVENS, ENGELBERT HUMPERDINCK, JIMI HENDRIX, THE CALIFORNIANS, THE QUOTATIONS & NICK JONES (COMPERE)

16 APRIL 1967

NICK HAIRS

This was another typical British package tour with a very varied line up. The main reason I was there was, of course, Jimi Hendrix. For me, he stole the show. I know I may be biased but he was just something special. He only did four or five numbers. There was no setting fire to his guitar as on a couple of previous shows on this tour. I had seen him for the first time at the Leicester Poly on 26th February 1967, and that gig just blew me away. The Walker Brothers were okay. There was a lot of screaming going on from the girls. Cat Stevens was okay too. I didn't bother with Englebert who closed the first half. I went to the bar!

JOHN RYDER

I was there and will never forget it. Jimi came on dragging his guitar across the stage floor. I remember some of the older audience members walked out when he started playing. He played 'Hey Joe', 'Wild Thing' and 'Purple Haze' and scraped his guitar across the front of his amp to get feedback. Awesome!

BARRY ROBINSON

I remember the screaming for the Walker Brothers was real loud! Jimi played 'Stone Free'!

ELIZABETH HENFREY

This may have been my first concert. I only went to see the Walker Brothers, and I had not heard of Jimi Hendrix. I thought he had his pyjamas on. But I was blown away.

BEV DAVIES

I was, and still am, a huge fan of the Walker Brothers. I always sat in the front row of the side balcony seats, so I could hang over the barrier and be closer to them. The support acts were great, although all we wanted were Scott, John and Gary to come on stage. We cried and screamed all the way through their performance. After the show, we went round to the stage door to await for them to come out, but we almost got run over by their car once as they raced off from fans. I had no voice for couple of days after through screaming at them so much. Happy days.

I actually met John Walker at Loughborough Town Hall a couple of years before he passed away. A lovely man. I still listen to their music now.

BLUES CARAVAN: SONNY TERRY & BROWNIE MCGHEE, SON HOUSE, MUDDY WATERS, SKIP JAMES, BUKKA WHITE, LITTLE WALTER, HOUND DOG TAYLOR, DILLARD CRUME, ODIE PAYNE & KOKO TAYLOR
22 OCTOBER 1967

STUART LANGFORD

My then brother-in-law gave me the ticket – it was probably the best thing he ever did – and I didn't really know what to expect. But I did have a ten-inch LP of Sonny Terry and Brownie McGee, one of whom was in a wheelchair and the other one was blind. They were on the bill, Son House and Muddy Waters were on the bill, and members of each band played with one another. So Little Walter played harmonica with somebody else for one of the numbers. It was a very relaxed, free-for-all evening, with the musicians swapping over roles and moving from one band to another.

The hall was full. It was just wonderful. It was all blues, it was all black, it was all real. It was strident and brilliant. I found out since that the compere was Joe Boyd, who went on to produce Pink Floyd and manage

GOIN' DOWN DE MONT: A PEOPLE'S HISTORY

Fairport Convention. He'd been sent over by an American production company to accompany all these musicians and shepherd them through England.

I went away and bought the Pye Golden Guinea *Rhythm & Blue All Stars* LP, which had Muddy Waters and Sonny Boy Williamson on it, and that and a couple of seminal albums got me interested in the blues then, and I am still interested in the blues now. But I had no idea at the time quite how legendary they were.

JOHN STRETTON

By 1967 I was heavily into blues music and had formed the Leicestershire Blues Appreciation Society and so was eager to sample the Blues Caravan at the Hall. It was sheer delight to see so many authentic blues greats, with my all-time favourites Son House, Skip James, Bukka White and Little Walter on show. I smuggled my camera inside to photograph as much as possible from the balcony seat.

Little Walter at De Mont

GOIN' DOWN DE MONT: A PEOPLE'S HISTORY

LED ZEPPELIN
13 MARCH 1969

STUART LANGFORD

Led Zeppelin played as part of Leicester University's rag week with Ferris Wheel and the Decoys as support. My mate Mick and I ran the disco that day; our speakers were tiny compared to everyone else's! The band arrived during the afternoon, and they were such nice guys. They hung around with us during the afternoon playing records from our rock selection – lots of Moby Grape and blues stuff – and then set up their equipment. No roadies in those days; they carried their own gear in from the van.

It was late afternoon, early evening, and Mick and I saw Jimmy Page kneeling on the stage. He'd opened one of the dips – they're the little hatches in the middle of the stage under which there are live sockets, so you don't need to run long cables across the stage, which is dangerous.

I heard this 'zzzzzzzz' noise, and saw Jimmy trying to wedge the bare ends of his amplifier lead into a 15-amp round socket under the stage. This was before the days of earth trips and RCD leakage devices that would cut the power off if you did anything stupid. For some reason, they'd taken the plugs off their amps and were just wedging the wires in with matchsticks.

So, there was Page, hardly able to see in the dark, reaching under the stage, feeling around, with the bare wires of his amplifier cable catching the odd spark, going 'zzzzzzzz' and with the smell of singeing in the air. I literally pulled him away. I can genuinely say he was within moments of electrocuting himself. And I said, 'Jimmy, don't do that! Mick and I will give you a plug for your amp.' So we gave him a round-pin plug from our toolbox of spares. And he said, 'Oh lads! Thanks ever so much. I'll give it you back at the end of the night.' Did he hell!

But they were fantastic. They played for three hours. Mick and I paid them, because we were a part of the college business side, 175 quid cash, and they held the money in their hands like school kids. 'Look at this, lads. We're rich! Let's go get egg and chips somewhere!'

I got their autographs, all except John Paul Jones. I eventually sold them to a Finnish journalist, and he met up with John Paul Jones and asked him to add his signature to the three. He got quite tearful remembering the days when the whole band was together.

JOHN MAYALL
9 NOVEMBER 1969

NICK HAIRS
The new Mayall band had no drummer, just Johnny Almond on saxes, Jon Mark on acoustic guitar and Steve Thompson on bass, with John Mayall singing and playing his usual guitar and harmonica. To be honest, I wasn't that impressed. Yeah, I bought the album, but I much preferred his previous line-ups. I lost all interest in John Mayall after this.

On a side note, during the intermission we noticed someone climbing the steps behind the stage. Making his way towards the organ. I recognized this man to be Zoot Money, so I shouted out 'Bruno!' – his middle name – from my seat in the front row of the balcony. He retorted back with 'Mother!' I think the stewards got him to climb down.

FAMILY AND EMILY MUFF
4 DECEMBER 1969

KATHY BUSHNELL
I co-founded the first female rock duo in Britain: Emily Muff. We toured extensively throughout the UK from 1968 to 1972, opening concerts for the band Family, who provided management and representation, and gave the duo its name. The first time we appeared at the De Montfort Hall was an extra special occasion. In addition to the honour of opening the show for Family in their hometown, my chick rock duo was to attend a post-gig party backstage to celebrate Family's latest album, *A Song for Me*, which was due to be released early the following year. To add to the excitement of that evening at the De Mont, scouts from Reprise, a major record label, were to be in the audience to audition us.

During our performance, flashbulbs were popping throughout our set.

After all, we were a rock and roll rarity: an all-female duo performing original numbers with vocal harmonies on Telecasters and Rickenbacker electric guitars and Hohner blues harmonicas. Prior to the post-gig party, I was mobbed in the hall by a crowd of Emily Muff fans. I signed numerous autographs for them, and I still recall how enthusiastic those Leicester fans were. I know I'll never forget them, or that special moment in time!

TAJ MAHALL & RARE BIRD
30 APRIL 1970

JOHN STRETTON

I was front row on a side balcony to witness and enjoy another favourite of mine, Taj Mahal, on the bill with Rare Bird for the princely sum of 15/-. Such was my excitement at Taj's music and performance that I was carried away, banging my arm on the balcony, in time to the music, to such an extent that I broke one of my cufflinks! Yes, I was at a Taj Mahal show wearing cufflinks!

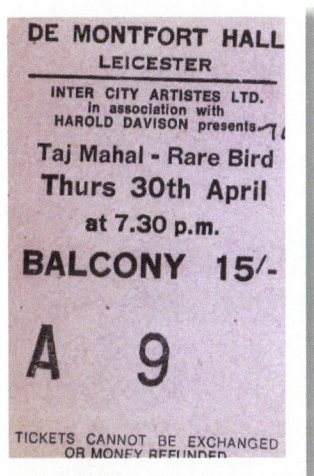

DEREK & THE DOMINOES, BRETT MARVIN & THE THUNDERBOLTS
21 SEPTEMBER 1970

NICK HAIRS

I was a fan of Eric Clapton and I had seen Cream and Blind Faith, so I made the effort to go to this gig. Was it worth it? Yes, but only just. They were a great band, don't get me wrong, but it was like they were all too tired. There weren't that many in the De Mont either. Bret Marvin and The Thunderbolts opened the show with a mix of blues.

TOM MURTHA
Even for a Cream fan, the gig was disappointing.

KEVIN HEWICK
I was 13 and thrilled to see Clapton in person. I wanted more huge, long guitar solos, but I liked the band! I've always thought that Eric's subdued mood was due to the death of Jimi Hendrix only three days before. They did a beautiful version of 'Little Wing', but not as a hastily put together tribute. They were already featuring it and had recorded it for the *Layla* album, from which they had broken off from during the sessions to do this rather oddly-timed UK tour. Of course there was no 'Layla' in the set itself. That was to be created later back at the recording studio with the slow end section stolen from Rita Coolidge.

CANNED HEAT & THE GROUNDHOGS
23 SEPTEMBER 1970

JOHN STRETTON
My excitement quotient was raised once more with the first visit to Leicester by Canned Heat, supported by The Groundhogs, still very much blues but of a whiter variety. I had been tipped off that Canned Heat were at the local Holiday Inn before the show. Asking at the desk if I could possibly speak to the group, I was amazed when Bob Hite, their singer and a mountain of a man, was standing next to me, asking how he could help. We had a half hour chat, and he was very ready to answer my questions. It seemed strange to next see him on stage, where he and the band performed with great enthusiasm and skill, but the performance did lack their former power, so soon after the death of Al Wilson, their slide guitar player and one of the musical powers of the group. They were also not helped by a lack of balance in their wall of sound, almost drowning Bob's vocals. Rather overshadowed by the US headliners, The Groundhogs did a fine job of performing their versions of the blues.

JETHRO TULL
28 SEPTEMBER 1970

RUPERT BOBROWICZ

As a young teenager I was delighted to attend, this being only 20 miles from where I lived. How excited was I? On the night Tull brought two support groups – a duo called Tír na nÓg and Procol Harum, who played some *Salty Dog* and 'Homburg' before ending with 'A Whiter Shade of Pale'. But it was Tull I had come see, and it wasn't too long before my expectations were met, then exceeded beyond measure.

I was in Seventh Heaven and more, because Tull were on stage before my very eyes: Ian Anderson complete with flute and chequered coat; Glenn Cornick with hair and bass; Clive Bunker with Tull drum kit; Martin Barre on lead guitar; and introducing 'Mr Ice Cream Man', John Evan, with Cheshire Cat smile and keyboards. What a fabulous set they played. Tull were on a high, Ian retorted, after their Isle of Wight concert. They were all buzzing. Songs from *This Was* and *Stand Up* greeted us, along with some bluesy numbers. Then came newer material, including 'With You There to Help Me', along with a long John Evan keyboard solo. Clive, Ian and John were all on form for the revised 'Dharma for One', which was akin to the live version on *Living in the Past*. 'My God' included a long-ish, exaggerated flute solo. 'For a Thousand Mothers' was well received, especially with its false ending, as was 'Nothing is Easy', while Glenn exceeded his bass solo on 'Bouree'.

FAMILY & AMERICA
1 DECEMBER 1970

JOHN STRETTON

This was the first show of Family's new tour with America as support. The US soft rock group took some time balancing their mics before they finally launched into their set, but their efforts were worthwhile, as their range of songs was near perfect. The crowd rewarded them with rapturous applause, which was impressive as all we really wanted were our local heroes.

Said heroes came straight out of the box with 'In My Own Time' and 'Part of the Load' without a wait, and the evening from one of my all-time favourite bands was a tremendous and fantastic send off for their forthcoming days on the road.

ADRIAN HAMMOND

As my first ever concert, I didn't know how encores worked, and at the end of Family's set, the band all went off stage. Then everyone started calling for more, so the band came back on and did another song. This repeated,

Family 1970 UK tour programme

and they came back a second time, and after a further song, they went off again. This time, the lights in the hall came on, and the equipment was switched off. Half the audience left the hall, but a significant number of people just kept on and on and on calling for more – basically refusing to leave. Eventually after about 20 minutes, the roadies came back onto stage, fired up the equipment and Family came back out for a third encore!

After that, I just assumed it would be the norm, but of course that situation never happened again at any gigs I attended.

WISHBONE ASH
14 JUNE 1971

ANDY BETTS

It fermented in 1970. I became a teenager that year, happily living in Oadby and obsessed with music. For my birthday, Mum and Dad bought me a second hand Dansette and I went to Brees Records in Oadby and bought my first single, 'Natural Sinner', by Fairweather, which I played to death and still own.

Back then, there were four or five weekly papers dedicated to music, the favourite of mine being *Melody Maker*, which introduced me to a new lingo of albums, bands, gigs, and venues. I noticed that there was a prescribed circuit of venues where the cream of rock bands played, places like the Colston Hall in Bristol, the Fairfield Halls in Croydon, the Free Trade Hall in Manchester and, of course, the De Montfort Hall (often misspelt as 'De Montford') in God's own city of Leicester.

My friend Julian had a proper stereo with Wharfedale speakers on which I heard a brilliant debut record by Wishbone Ash, whose twin guitars I found irresistible, and as we moved into 1971, Julian informed me that Wishbone Ash were to play live at De Mont in June. I coughed up the ticket money from my paper round and Julian went down Northampton Square to the municipal box office and came back to Oadby with the treasured tickets.

I had never been to a live gig, and after an agonising wait, the day duly arrived. Julian and I were dropped off at those hallowed gates on Granville Road courtesy of my dad's Renault 4. The fading light of the summer evening framed the beautiful frontage of this special place that always reminds you that you are on a night out. I had butterflies then and still do now whenever I go there.

We were too young to use the bar, so we went directly to our seats, eight rows from the front. The lights dimmed and the support band, Glencoe, took to the stage. As they hit that first chord, a lightbulb went off in my head that this glorious noise was not coming from either my humble Dansette or Julian's more upmarket rig. No, this was live music actually played twenty feet in front of me. I was utterly mesmerised by that and by the Hall itself, which seemed to be from another planet.

I have no idea if Glencoe were actually any good. I cannot remember the music itself. It was the experience that absorbed me

After roadies had stripped the stage of Glencoe's kit and assembled

Wishbone's beautiful backline Orange amps, there was a short wait before the moment arrived. The band hit the stage and played most of that great debut album. This was utterly brilliant – not just live music, but material that I knew and loved so well that brought me to my feet and had me standing on my seat moving to the magic.

The band were ecstatically received, and the audience demanded two encores, the second of which was 'Where Were You Tomorrow', at the conclusion of which Martin Turner, the bassist, thanked us for being a great audience and informed us that the gig had been recorded live and that we had all gone down on record.

Martin was good to his word because when the band's superb second album, *Pilgrimage*, saw the light of day in September 1971, the sleeve notes confirmed the final track was recorded live at De Montfort Hall, Leicester on 14 June 1971.

My first unforgettable gig at the best venue there is for live music survives for all time on record, and the pubescent cheers of the 13-year-old me are somewhere in the mix!

TRAFFIC & PAUL RODGERS' PEACE
20 SEPTEMBER 1971

NICK HAIRS
My memory is a bit sketchy. It was a very loose gig but enjoyable. Paul Rogers' Peace was blues-based, with Rodgers playing a Fender Strat and on vocals. Peace only did about a dozen or so gigs.

KEVIN HEWICK
I went with my dad. I was 14. Rodgers used two Fender Strats – I think he said one had been adapted in Japan to have an extra D string. I remember them being rather like a poor man's Free. One song was called 'Lady': 'She was a lady/She was right on yeah.' Nothing to worry Bob Dylan there! Traffic were very loose. The expanded line up including Leicester's very own Ric Grech on bass. I was in awe of their core of Winwood, Capaldi and Wood. I'd been a big fan of their *John Barleycorn Must Die* album.

On a personal note, after the show because when my dad and I got home, my mum got a call from a hospice in London, where my grandma passed away that evening aged 49.

T.REX
8 NOVEMBER 1971

JOHN LANGHAM
By the time T.Rex appeared at the De Montfort Hall, Marc Bolan and the band had three hit singles under their belt and a huge fan following to match The Beatles visits just eight years earlier. This time, Marc was promoting his new album, calling the tour *Electric Warrior* and plugging his new single, 'Jeepster', released just three days earlier.

I had been freelancing for the BBC for some time, covering many concerts at the De Montfort Hall, and thanks to the City Entertainments Manager, I was permitted to park my car at the rear of the Hall, entering through the stage door, hence my tickets were never cancelled.

I recorded a great interview with Marc, covering many aspects from when he was a washer-up at a Wimpey bar right through to when he changed his style from acoustic to electric guitar. He gave me a wonderful quote which I have never forgotten: 'Everything I do is primarily for my own pleasure; if someone else likes it, I feel very honoured.'

When we had finished the interview, all his band mates had disappeared, and so he asked me if I could give him a lift to his hotel. I told him that I would but there was a problem – my car was just behind several hundred girls all chanting his name. 'No problem,' he said, 'I'll get into your sheepskin Afghan coat with you and we'll walk round the side of the hall to it!'

I was fearful that not only Marc but I, too, would be torn apart, but he was adamant that he had done this sort of thing before. So we went out from the dressing room into the main auditorium, where people were still leaving, with four legs poking out of the bottom of my coat. We continued out through the main entrance and walked down the side of the Hall and calmly got into my car. We drove through the crowd and thankfully nobody noticed my valuable consignment, which I duly delivered to the Grand Hotel.

JOHN STRETTON

This was my first exposure to Marc Bolan's T.Rex, to pre-pubescent screaming and to people standing on the seats. Happily, I was again in the front balcony (a 60p ticket!) with a clear view. I had liked him as Tyrannosaurus Rex but was not enamoured of his new persona.

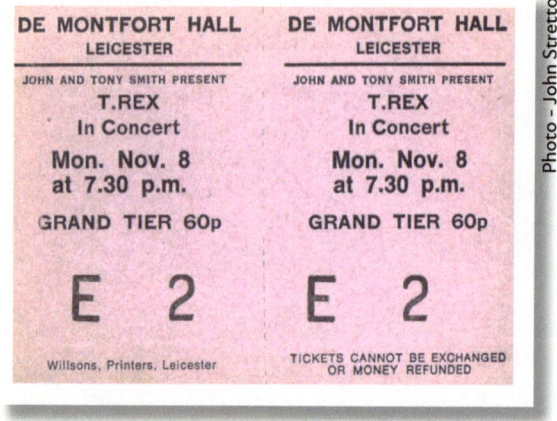

LORRAYNE WILKINSON

I was with my then boyfriend, Michael Daly. Michael was a Leicester lad studying at Leeds College of Art, as was I (a Leeds girl). We travelled down to Leicester for the day just for the concert. We had been fans since Tyrannosaurus Rex days and had front row seats. We were very surprised to be surrounded by screaming teenage girls who were obviously influenced by T.Rex's chart success.

ELTON JOHN
24 NOVEMBER 1971

NEIL HARRIS

Before coming to Leicester to study, I had always been envious of the concert venues available (De Montfort Hall, Granby Halls, Leicester University and De Montfort University when it was Leicester Polytechnic) and the bands they regularly attracted to Leicester. The Elton John concert was the first major concert I ever went to. Elton John had a meteoric rise in profile at this time. There was a lot of resentment from UK rock journalists because much of the excitement was being

GOIN' DOWN DE MONT: A PEOPLE'S HISTORY

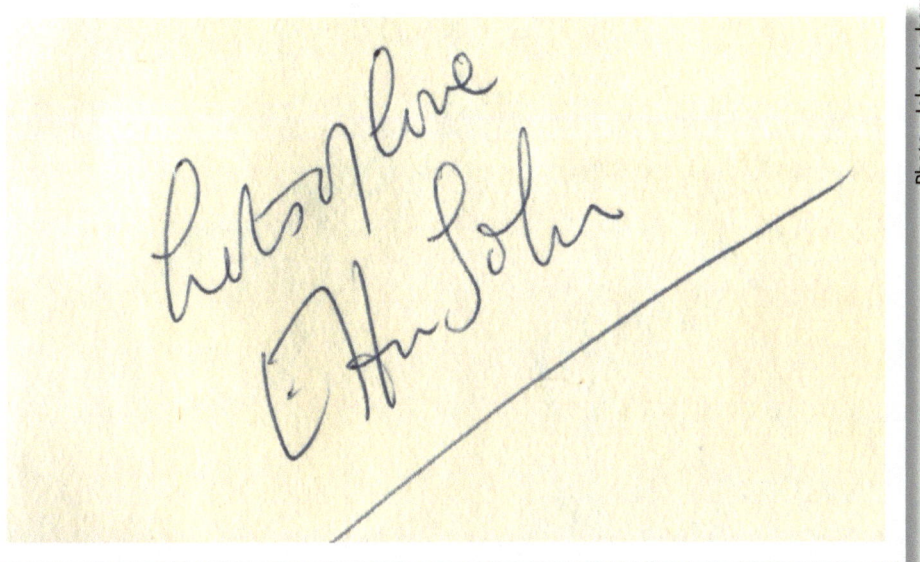

Photo - John Langham

Elton John's autograph

generated on the other side of the pond. I even recall his management actually defending him on the *Old Grey Whistle Test*. I can't recall he had any input. He let his music talk for him.

I was not sure what to expect. I had heard and enjoyed tracks from *Tumbleweed Connection* but apart from the *Old Grey Whistle Test* I had never seen him play live. The evening started slowly. England Dan and John Ford Coley were the support act. They were unfortunately not my kind of music at all – so not a great start.

Then Elton came on accompanied by Dee Murray and Nigel Olsson. He really hit the ground running with high energy performances of songs from the album the tour was promoting, *Madman Across the Water*, as well as songs from *Tumbleweed Connection* and some earlier material such as 'Your Song'. I recall a few rock and roll numbers also being thrown in at some stage.

The show went down brilliantly with a packed audience. No hype here. The stage was fairly bare – just the band. Elton didn't need a light show and special effects to generate excitement – his performance did that. Next morning my first stop was a record store to buy the album.

This concert was the start of a love affair with De Montfort Hall.

GOIN' DOWN DE MONT: A PEOPLE'S HISTORY

BLACK SABBATH
1 FEBRUARY 1972

RICH BARTON, DIESEL PARK WEST

My everlasting memory of Black Sabbath (apart from thinking Ozzy looked a bit overweight) is the next day at school. Whenever my teeth touched, it sounded like a bell going off in my head. I couldn't hear anything for a while. It was the first time I had seen such an array of Marshall stacks. Geezer's bass was literally thumping you in the chest every time he played a note.

PINK FLOYD
10 FEBRUARY 1972

NEIL HARRIS

I had been looking forward to seeing Pink Floyd live for many years. And this was the first opportunity to do so. My fear was that the industrial troubles at the time – power outages, frequent blackouts – would kill the concert before it even stated and, if it started, would it even finish.

Cover to the lyric sheet handed out to the Pink Floyd audience

I had heard about the new Pink Floyd revolutionary sound system and the light shows were already a key feature of all of their performances, so I was really up for this one.

The show began with the Pink Floyd heartbeat travelling around the concert hall and wrapping around the audience – this was really impressive and left the audience in anticipation for what was to follow. I then sat amongst a full house of loyal followers eagerly braced for all my favourite tracks to be belted out. This didn't happen.

Floyd were taking an innovative new work out on the road. This soon-to-be album was being road tested in performance throughout this tour, and refined as the tour and performances progressed. In hindsight, it would now be cool to say that I was immediately won over by this new offering and knew it would set the standard for the next two decades, but sadly that was not the case. The reality was I felt a little cheated. Where was all the good stuff? Who starts a concert with a completely new work? There was no sign of anything I wanted to hear or recognised until the end.

The piece finished, and afterward some of the tracks I knew well and wanted to hear were played splendidly. The sound system (I think it was quad sound) fired out some wonderful musical and abstract sound effects throughout the whole evening. I don't recall any significant power issues but recall there were maybe some small issues.

The musicianship of the band was as always superb and the concert in hindsight unique – a real major event. The new piece being played and refined was *The Dark Side of the Moon: A Place for Assorted Lunatics*. At the concert, a set of lyrics was left on each seat to give the audience some sense of what they were about to see and hear. Since the concert, I have played this album more than any other I possess and now feel quite guilty for my original indifference.

Sadly, in those days there was rarely any visual or even audio evidence of rock group concert performances apart from the occasional dodgy bootleg. It would be great to replay the evening to see where I went wrong!

JOHN LANGHAM

I guess this concert was one of my most memorable. The tour was promoting their latest release, *Meddle*, but they were trying things out at their one and only appearance at the De Montfort Hall. The current hi-fi trend was for quadraphonic record releases – using surround sound with speakers to the rear as well as the front and also maintaining clearly defined left and right sound channels. While this may be straightforward to produce in the studio, Pink Floyd wanted to go that step further and perform the surround experience in the theatre, so there were speakers behind the audience as well as the front of house.

Having performed excerpts from the *Meddle* album and the classic 'Careful With That Axe, Eugene' (complete with a screaming axe-wielding girl in a nightdress running across the stage), an intermission followed.

During the intermission, lyric sheets were distributed for a new piece of music in preparation for their next album. The title had not been finalised, nor had it even recorded yet. They wanted to call it *The Dark Side of the Moon*, but a band called Medicine Head had beaten them to it with that title. So, they had a plan B – a title of *A Piece for Assorted Lunatics*. They ultimately determined that Medicine Head seemed a one-hit-wonder and proceeded with their first choice of title when they recorded the album later in 1972.

So the De Montfort Hall was treated to an early performance, in full quadraphonic sound, of *The Dark Side of the Moon* before it had even been recorded. I particularly recall the track 'Money' was performed with a soundtrack of Malcolm Muggeridge, the journalist and TV social critic, spouting a section of a sermon about the evils of money from the front, whilst the quadraphonic soundtrack depicted a church collection plate being passed down the rows from left to right. The sound passed right through you as the chink of money dropped into the plate and passed to the rows behind. This was changed to become cash registers ringing on the final album recording.

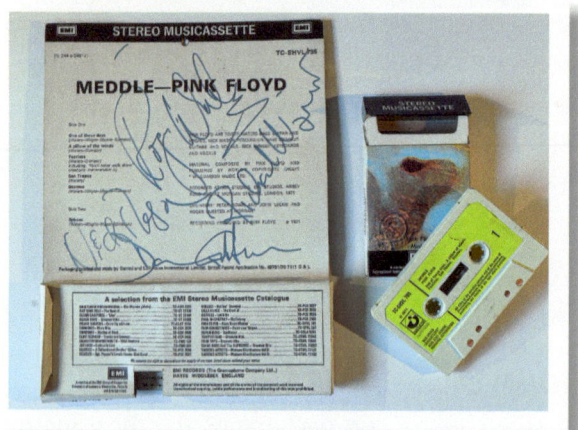

Photos - John Langham

Autographed Pink Floyd cassette in its original packaging

I was granted an interview and was also able to obtain a full set of autographs on my cassette sleeve of *Meddle*. The cassette was slipped into a flip-top packet and inserted into a seven-inch laminated mini album sleeve – a short-lived method of packaging, which obviously became too expensive to continue marketing that way.

It was a truly memorable experience and historic event.

KEVIN HEWICK

I was in the fourth row of the stalls with my dad and my uncle, who got a cassette recorder in and taped it! They took ages between songs tuning up, with no stage chat, wearing long hair jeans and t-shirts and looking like roadies. 'Echoes' was over 28 minutes and truly astounding.

DAVE HARRIMAN

I was there at this fantastic show. They did 'Careful With That Axe, Eugene' as an encore. A big orange revolving light to the left of the stage went off to coincide with the scream. I nearly fell off my seat!

THE MOODY BLUES
27 FEBRUARY 1972

NEIL HARRIS

They were due to play the De Mont on 5 November 1971, but they cancelled a chunk of that tour due to John Lodge being ill. Then they were due to play at the University on March 1, but I think the two concerts were merged into one date. This was only time I can ever recall an artist – I think it was Mike Pinder – leaving the concert halfway through a set to take a leak. He even told the audience first. You kind of remember strange stuff like that.

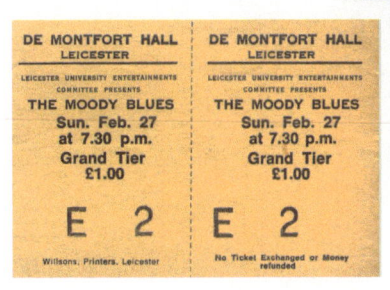

Moody Blues ticket and signed programme

GOIN' DOWN DE MONT: A PEOPLE'S HISTORY

JETHRO TULL
14 MARCH 1972

JOHN RABONE

The usual mode of entry, via guitar string and fire door, failed for once, and so a bunch of us loitered with intent. Spotting an open ground floor window on the left side near the back, one of our group tried to climb in, not realising that this was probably the artist's toilet. Then a massive, maned head appeared at the window and roared angrily. This turned out to be Ian Anderson, singer and flautist with Jethro Tull, who were headlining that evening. That was one of the few evenings when I failed to get in.

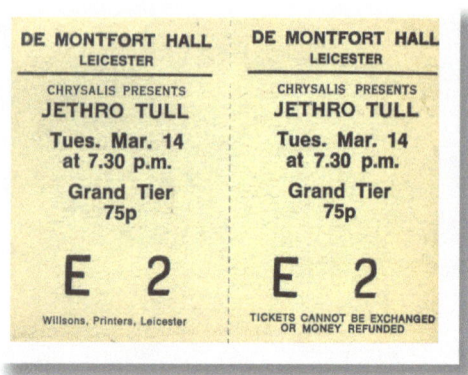
Photo - John Langham

NEIL HARRIS

I remember this concert much more for audience interaction than content. This tour was to promote *Thick as a Brick*. Sadly, the anticipation of each Jethro Tull record or concert was for me always greater than what was actually delivered. Maybe that says more about me than the band. By the time of this concert, Tull had effectively become an American band culturally, and they played the role perfectly.

The whole of *Thick as a Brick* kicked off the show, which was well received though it was not too familiar to the audience at this time. This was followed by 'Aqualung' and other earlier popular tracks, and then an interminable, mind-numbing collection of instrumental pieces with Ian Anderson going into his full flute persona. This section seemed to go on forever, and you could see many in the audience getting more and more bored. Ian Anderson however seemed to be really enjoying it.

Then – a magical moment. Halfway through yet another marathon flute solo, Anderson thankfully stopped to take a breath and stared at the audience awaiting the whooping and hollering he anticipated but which did not materialise. He then admonished the audience saying in disbelief that this bit always went down really well in America. At this point, a voice from the floor shouted back, 'Well fuck off back there then!'

It's terrible that this is a highlight of a concert you have watched!

CAPTAIN BEEFHEART
30 MARCH 1972

STUART LANGFORD

My wife turned me onto Beefheart's records when we started going out together in Sunderland. We saw him in Newcastle and met him backstage, then kind of followed the tour around and saw him again at the De Mont. *Spotlight Kid* was the current album. He had Rockette Morton on bass, and the drummer had a pair of ladies' panties stretched over his head with his hair coming out like mad pigtails through the leg holes.

Jimmy Carl Black from the Mothers of Invention was there, and we met him and Captain Beefheart backstage. He was such a nice man.

DAVE HARRIMAN

I was somewhere near the front. It was an amazing show. It started, I think, with a ballet dancer, then a belly dancer. After that, Rockette Morton played his brilliant bass solo. I remember someone in the audience behind me was laughing

Captain Beefheart ticket & signed programme

hysterically in between the songs when Don was talking. The guy was forcing himself to be crazy for some reason. Don said, 'Who brought the hyena in?' Then he said, 'I don't believe in insanity, just varying degrees of misconnection.' I think that shut the guy up. It was one of the best shows down the De Mont.

DEEP PURPLE
12 SEPTEMBER 1972

DAVID BRIGGS
The first real band I ever saw live was Deep Purple. Actually, strictly speaking, Deep Purple's support band was the first, a superb outfit called Glencoe. At the time, the De Montfort Hall was one of those 'big' venues that everyone played at (even The Beatles).

In the bar before the gig, as a 'cool' 16 year old, I got chatting to a guy with long hair. I asked him if he had ever seen Deep Purple before. He said, 'I've heard them many times, but never paid to see them live.' I replied, 'You are gonna love this man.'

Here's the embarrassing bit: The guy with the long hair that I had been chatting to, unbeknown to me of course, was in fact Ian Paice, Deep Purple's drummer.

LINDISFARNE & GENESIS
12 OCTOBER 1972

NEIL HARRIS
Undoubtedly some of the most memorable concerts I was lucky enough to attend at De Montfort Hall were headlined either by Genesis or former front man Peter Gabriel. The growth of Genesis from playing smaller venues (usually as part of a Charisma bands showcase) to selling out major venues such as De Montfort Hall took only twelve months and can be demonstrated via three Leicester concerts – two of them at De Montfort Hall.

I stumbled upon Genesis by accident at their 23 February 1972 show at Leicester Polytechnic, an infamous show due to crowd trouble. The problems were caused by a bunch of bikers who caused chaos hurling glasses and bottles, which were smashing around the place. Lack of any more readily available beer was the root cause of their unhappiness. One or two band members took away particles of glass on their clothing as a souvenir of the visit.

But by the time of their first De Montfort Hall concert, I had become very familiar with their major early albums by the time – *Trespass*, *Nursery Cryme* and *Foxtrot*.

This concert was yet another Charisma showcase, opened by Rab Noakes. Genesis were next up, followed by Lindisfarne, who were probably at the peak of their popularity at this time. Genesis were outstanding, with Peter Gabriel clearly running the show. To be honest, the rest of the band seemed to fade into the background. The first signs of their theatricality emerged in the set, with Gabriel appearing in a flowing red dress wearing a fox's head, just like the cover of their fourth album, *Foxtrot*, which they were promoting. This drew a few gasps.

Lindisfarne autumn 1972 UK tour programme & ticket

They stole the show. I am sure that a number of bemused Geordies, who had come to see their hometown heroes Lindisfarne and who were topped up with Newcastle Brown Ale, struggled with the concept.

FAMILY
29 JANUARY 1973

RICH BARTON

I was a 15-year-old schoolboy (Lancaster Boys Secondary Modern). Me and my mates were lapping up all the new (to us) sounds that were happening in the early Seventies. Family came on the radar – we loved 'The Weaver's Answer' and 'In My Own Time'. An added bonus is they were a Leicester band. We had to see them!

They did not disappoint. They were mind blowing, electrifying, and LOUD. Tony Ashton's organ began the show, filtering through the dry ice, and then – bang! – the band were in with 'Top of the Hill'. Brilliant… double-neck guitars, throat-ripping vocals, unusual and inventive songs, and great musicianship.

Roger threw his tambourine out into the crowd after nearly putting his fist through it. I jumped up and got it! I still have it. A budding photographer friend, Phil Zara, took the picture.

Top: Family on stage. Middle: Chappo's tambourine. Bottom: Family ticket

NEIL HARRIS

There could be few more unpredictable and aggravating bands than Family. I was, and am, a real fan and have accumulated all their recordings. I also believe that they were probably the most underrated recording band of the 1970s. Sadly, going to see them was always a bit like playing musical Russian roulette.

I only saw the band play once at the De Montfort Hall – a great set list but, if I'm honest, only average delivery. Chappo's voice, which is consistently strong and unique on record, can sound very thin live, which it did on this occasion. There were some highlights such as 'Burlesque' and 'My Friend the Sun'. The audience reacted well to both and they ended up as singles from the *Bandstand* album.

As you would expect from a successful local band, they had a large enthusiastic following and were well received by the audience. The friend I went with told me that this show was the best he had seen them play. I am used to being in a minority and felt it was long way from being their best performance. But there was never a dull moment.

The tour coincided with the release of *Bandstand* which is one of my favourite albums from the band. At the show their promotion team handed out a flyer for 'My Friend the Sun', which was then their latest single.

Their farewell performance was at the end of '73 at Leicester Polytechnic, and part of the band (Roger Chapman and Charlie Whitney) re-emerged as Streetwalkers, who also played the De Montfort Hall in 1977. Both were great concerts. Family's music has not dated and still sounds fresh.

GENESIS
25 FEBRUARY 1973

NEIL HARRIS

A year on from the Leicester Poly gig, Genesis had grown from a minor band playing small venues to being a theatre-filling act. This concert was spectacular with their dramatic music merged with superb theatrical effects and lighting. Gabriel was the master showman and had the audience in the palm of his hands. It was staggering that the band had got so popular in the space of twelve months.

GOIN' DOWN DE MONT: A PEOPLE'S HISTORY

This concert was recorded for transmission on American radio as part of a *King Biscuit Flower Hour* promotion. Charisma also decided to release the concert as a budget priced album – *Genesis Live* – to bridge the gap between *Foxtrot* and the next album release, *Selling England by the Pound*. Peter Gabriel apparently strongly resisted its release but eventually relented. The album was also released in the US to showcase the band. The band had no idea before the concert that it was going to appear on an album.

I met with Steve Hackett many years later who confirmed this. It is ironic that this is now considered to be one of the classic live albums of the period.

All the tracks on the album, with the exception of 'Return of the Giant Hogweed', were from the Leicester concert. The only non-Leicester track was recorded at Manchester Free Trade Hall a day earlier. At the Leicester concert, a free flexi disc was handed out at the door of a track that did not make the *Foxtrot* album – 'Twilight Alehouse'.

When I met up with Steve Hackett years later, he kindly signed the cover for me, and we spent some time discussing the album's history. De Montfort Hall was a favoured venue of many bands.

Genesis ticket from 1973

Neil Harris (right) discussed the genesis of *Genesis Live* with Steve Hackett

STEVE HACKETT, GENESIS

The recording [of the album *Genesis Live*] was suggested by our American publicist, Nancy Lewis, to be part of the *King Biscuit Flower Hour* [an influential syndicated US radio show] tradition, which had been so successful promoting British acts. Genesis was doing so many shows at that time, there was little time available for recording. Charisma put it out as a stop gap.

[The album] was recorded at the De Montfort Hall because the acoustics sounded particularly live in that venue. The audience's reaction to the opening chords of 'Watcher of the Skies' was interesting. The crowd shouted out 'Hooray!' at the beginning. After that, all the crowds did the same thing. The drums sounded particularly good on that album. It wasn't easy to get a live drum sounding so good. We also felt that the mellotron sounded better there than on the *Foxtrot* studio album.

It was a rough and ready performance without the pressure of feeling we were recording a live album. It was only decided later to turn it into an album.

STATUS QUO
2 APRIL 1973

BRUCE PEGG

At the time, Quo had just released *Piledriver*, the album that completed their transformation from 1960s psychedelic one-hit wonders to the hard-driving boogie band that became so massively successful later on. 'Paper Plane' was in the charts – it was the only song of theirs that I knew, but I was so excited to go to my first rock concert that I didn't really care.

What persuaded me to go was probably the ticket price: 45p (50p if you bought one after 1 April, when VAT was introduced for the first time in the UK). At that time, most concert tickets were around £1.00, or the amount of money I earned in one week on my paper round. So, that made tickets for the show pretty cheap even by the standards of the day – reason enough to hop on the 67 bus and head up Evington Road to the De Mont.

I remember the light show, primitive even in those days, consisted of about a dozen red-gelled PAR 64s that came on at the beginning of each song, flashed a bit, and went off at the end. And the stage show, such as it was, mostly involved the band draping long hair over guitars, just like the *Piledriver* album

GOIN' DOWN DE MONT: A PEOPLE'S HISTORY

cover. Once in a while, however, Messrs Parfitt and Rossi would walk to opposite sides of the stage and run full tilt at each other in a game of chicken that had the road crew scrambling to untangle leads after every song.

While the band was still playing their last song – probably 'Roadhouse Blues' – my friend Jimmy and I looked in horror at our watches. It was just a few minutes before 11pm. We ran out of there and began legging it down Granville Road to the corner of London Road and Evington Road where we could catch the 67 at around 11.05pm, five minutes after it left the town centre. It was the first of many such sprints, as missing the bus meant a sheepish call home to Mum and Dad, and a very long and potentially dodgy walk back to Evington followed by a week without seeing your friends. Needless to say, we didn't miss it very often.

From then on, I was hooked on going to see rock shows there whenever I could scrounge up the money to do so.

Francis Rossi of Status Quo

Status Quo 1973 UK tour programme, ticket and autographs

PAUL CANNY

My first gig at the De Mont was Quo, and they still had seating in the stalls which confined the inevitable melee of headbanging to a narrow strip of space between the front row and the stage, and down the centre aisle. It wasn't many moons later that the seating was removed for rock concerts, only reappearing for more refined acts such as Ralph McTell and Renaissance.

FOCUS
6 MAY 1973

BRUCE PEGG

This was my second show, and I probably went expecting the kind of energy I had seen at the Status Quo show. I was sadly disappointed. The band just stood there and played their instruments. They played their big hits 'Sylvia' and 'Hocus Pocus', which were fine, but they encored by repeating 'Hocus Pocus' three or four more times. It seemed like forever. I was only 13, but I was becoming a music critic already!

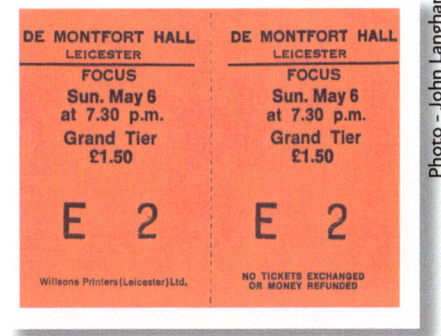

DAVID BOWIE
11 JUNE 1973

BRUCE PEGG

My Mum stood in line at the De Mont box office to get the David Bowie tickets, as I would have been in school when they went on sale. I remember they sold out immediately, and I couldn't believe my luck that I was actually going to see one of my idols.

Ever the showman, Bowie knew how to wind up an audience before he even set foot on stage. There was no warmup act, and the 8pm start time came and went. By 8.15pm, the crowd was getting very restless, and

GOIN' DOWN DE MONT: A PEOPLE'S HISTORY

by 8.30pm you could positively feel the tension. I was with my friend Mal West, sitting in the stalls somewhere under the balcony, when the houselights finally went off; the band broke into 'Hang on to Yourself', and the audience in the stalls charged the stage. The chairs that had been in orderly rows just seconds before went flying, and people just started scrambling for the best vantage points.

Photo – John Langham

Instinctively, Mal and I ran down the centre aisle from our seats at the back of the stalls and got to about row G or so when the crush of people got so thick we couldn't move any further forward. All the chairs in front of us had been destroyed or kicked to the side of the hall by then, but we found a couple that were still intact and stood on them for the entire show. We figured that no jobsworth would come anywhere near us and tell us to sit down after that little melee.

To the best of my recollection, that was the last time the De Mont put seats in the stalls during the Seventies or Eighties for anything they deemed to be a rock concert.

What followed was close to two hours of rock and roll perfection. The costume changes, the mime routines, the sheer power of the music – everything deliberately calculated to overwhelm the senses. Toward the end, during 'The Jean Genie', Bowie and Mick Ronson even simulated sex on stage, and though my 13-year-old mind didn't know exactly was going on, I had a pretty good idea.

I was gobsmacked by it all. It was just about the coolest thing I ever saw or ever will see again.

Afterwards, we went to the backstage door. There were only a handful of people there, so we stuck around for a while to see if we could get an autograph. But all we got was a fleeting glimpse of Mr. Bowie being hurriedly escorted into a waiting Rolls-Royce. I remember thinking at the time that it wouldn't have killed him to spend five minutes with his fans. But this was at the height of Ziggy mania, so I am sure that there were plenty of crazies out there that he wanted to avoid.

GOIN' DOWN DE MONT: A PEOPLE'S HISTORY

ANDY BETTS

The alarm clock awakened my 15-year-old self on a spring morning in 1973, at home in Oadby. It was 5am, a good hour earlier even than the crazy hour I would normally get up to do my paper round. I went to my brother's room and shook him to life, reminding him we were leaving for Leicester in half an hour. After a coffee and a call in sick to excuse me from my round, we set off, meeting two mates at the top of Brabazon Road.

We walked through Oadby and into leafy Knighton and Stoneygate sustained by an illicit pack of Embassy Regal. We had to walk (the Midland Red buses did not start running from Oadby until later than we could risk). Vicky Park came into view at 6.30am and we made Northampton Square dead on 6.45am as we intended to join the large queue snaking into Charles Street. After what seemed an eternity, but in reality was probably not more than a couple of hours, we were in the old municipal box office and each had a ticket for David Bowie at De Montfort Hall in June.

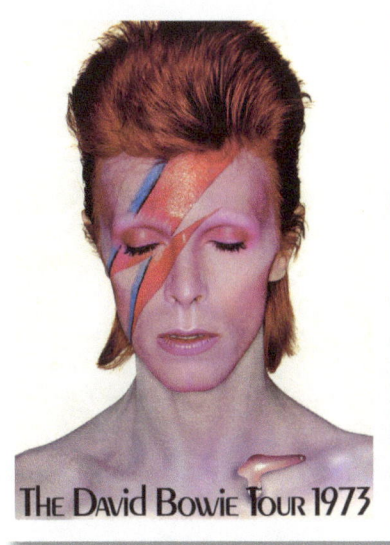

David Bowie 1973 UK tour programme

I painted my 'green flash' silver for the Starman; yes, I really was that sad! My brother Simon, on the other hand, opted for faded denim dungarees worn with nothing underneath so one nil to him in the cool stakes.

The show, Simon and I still agree, was the best thing we ever saw on stage – two hours, five costume changes and the very best of what the great man had to offer at that point.

I am sure if you talk to anyone present on that night they will have the same opinion; it was the gig of a lifetime. Those of us who loved Bowie are gutted at his passing in a way that non-believers can never understand. He, for me, was the man that opened my eyes to all art in a way my teachers never could.

It is true to say that every book I have chosen to read, every painting admired, every play, show, ballet and gig that I have attended since that June evening in 1973 owe something to it for the beautiful spark it ignited.

Thank you, David, your show was life-changing and life-enhancing and it took place in the city I love.

GOIN' DOWN DE MONT: A PEOPLE'S HISTORY

JOHN STRETTON
Avante garde is the phrase I would apply to David Bowie. This was my first experience with him, but this time I was in the stalls, in the midst of the screaming and seat standing. Alien to this 39-year-old, it was not something I either enjoyed or thought to be appropriate to someone who had so much talent on display.

JOHN CHAPMAN
It was the *Aladdin Sane* tour; tickets were £1.25. I was only eight rows back in the centre aisle seats – about the ideal position for the sound and visuals relative to the sound desk – but it took no time for the crowd to get up and run to the front, so I was up there like a shot. I was pretty much right at the stage, maybe one row of people in front of me so for nearly all of the gig. Bowie was only feet away from me when centre stage. He went through a lot of costume changes. He came right up to where I was, so I managed to touch his foot for a second. Real fan stuff I guess. It was an amazing show.

MARTIN PAGE
My dad worked at the Grand Hotel, and in 1973 his mate's daughter asked if he could nip round to Town Hall Square and pick up some tickets for David Bowie, which he agreed to do. He went expecting to take five minutes out of work, as he'd never heard of Bowie, and ended queuing for hours with what he described as 'weirdos'. He was taken aback by men in makeup, folk with brightly coloured clothes, Ziggy haircuts, etc.

The funny thing is they were laughing at him the entire time, as he was dressed in full morning suit – dark pinstripe jacket, light grey trousers and sensible shoes. If only there were mobile cameras around then. He actually said those that spoke to him were really nice people – why wouldn't they be?

ANDREW BARTLETT
There were problems with the sound and the electrics all night. He was late on, and because of all the hassle, he went off at 10.30pm and didn't return. To make matters worse, a moron a little further down our row thought it was clever to work up a head on a bottle of Newcastle Brown and then spray everyone with it. From bad to worse, you might say!

ROY WOOD'S WIZZARD
25 JUNE 1973

JOHN CHAPMAN

They sounded just like their records – so good they could play the stuff from memory. But they didn't even play for an hour. We were most disappointed at the length of the show.

GARY GLITTER
26 JUNE 1973

TONY WIGHTMAN

I didn't go, but on the evening of the 26th, I was making my way home after seeing friends in Wigston. I got off the bus on University Road near to the school. I was just crossing the road when I was almost struck by a fast-moving Rolls-Royce. Sat in the back? You've guessed: the sparkly one, if somewhat tarnished now!

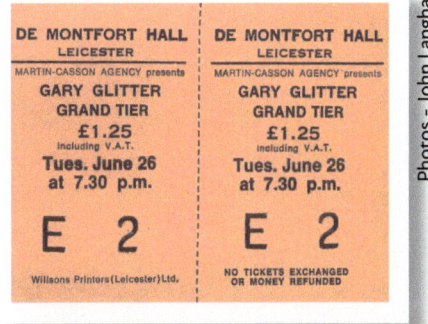

CARL LIQUORISH

I went with some mates, for a laugh. He forgot words that an amoeba could remember, dropped the microphone and trod on it, and had various costume changes. I recall him saying, 'Do you like my outfit? You should do – you paid for it!' I also

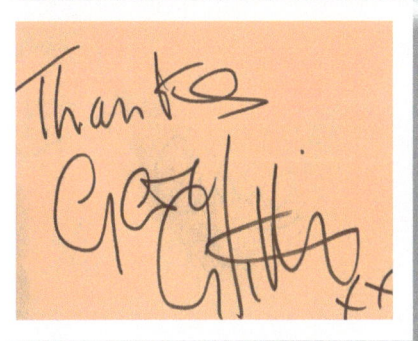

Gary Glitter ticket and autograph

recall a young woman standing on her chair behind me. She grabbed my (then) long hair and was jumping up and down holding it. I kicked the chair from under her to teach her a lesson.

We left early and went to the pub.

GOIN' DOWN DE MONT: A PEOPLE'S HISTORY

HAWKWIND
16 JULY 1973

BRUCE PEGG

Hawkwind played the De Mont many times in the Seventies. On this occasion, they were still performing 'The Space Ritual', a sensory assault of mind-numbing metal music with psychedelic backdrop projections, a naked dancer and enough strobe lighting to induce an epileptic fit. For its time, it was groundbreaking, even though it may have induced the tinnitus that I still have fifty years on!

STEPHEN HILL

At the end of the show, we go round to the back of the hall to the stage door to see the band, as you do when you are a kid. All of a sudden, the door gets kicked open, and some great big hairy Hell's Angel-looking guy comes

Hawkwind's *Space Ritual* album with the original packaging addressed to Stephen Hill

running out of there with a girl in his arms. And he says, 'Who knows the way to the hospital?'

So, Mr Do-Gooder here goes, 'Oh, I know where the hospital is, mate.' There's this great big American car behind us – massive great thing – and this great big hairy lemon throws the girl in the back seat, grabs hold of me and says, 'Right, come on! Show me where the hospital is.' And this is at 11pm. I was on a curfew, and the last bus was in five minutes. If I didn't get it, I had to walk, and it was about three or four miles back to Evington.

So I jumped in this motor and leave all my mates behind. And this girl wasn't very well – she was looking a bit touch-and-go to be honest. And this fellow goes up the road past my school, the Wyggeston Boys. He gets to the top of the road, and we need to turn right to get to the Leicester Royal Infirmary. And there's a great big No Right Turn sign there. And I said 'Oh, sorry, you can't turn right here.' And he says, 'Fuck off!' and just turned right in this great big American car.

We get to the Royal Infirmary and they rush her in there. Now the girl's name was Stacia, and the bloke driving the car was none other than Lemmy. And eventually he comes back out and I said, 'How's the young girl?'

And he starts looking at me – he's from a different world from me, he's no middle-class, 14-year-old kid – like I'm a right plonker. And he says, 'Give me your name and address. We'll send you an album.'

And I said, 'Well, I better phone my dad,' because by now it's about 2am. And I got him out of bed, which went down like a lead balloon, and he came and picked me up.

So I got home and got a bollocking off my mum and dad. But a few weeks later, I got a package in the post from Hawkwind's office in Notting Hill, London. And it was an album, signed by the whole band, and all these years later, I've still got it with the original postage stamps on it!

THE KINKS
20 SEPTEMBER 1973

RICH BARTON
As a kid in the Sixties, I had always been a big fan of their singles. Even though I am a Beatle nut, the Kinks were possibly the greatest singles band. The De Mont show was slightly sad. It wasn't full, and there was lots of space downstairs. But they were always a great band live, with Dave Davies on guitar. Ray Davies seemed distant; he may have been pissed, and at one point he tripped over the monitor and fell flat on his face. That could have been intentional for effect, but I'm not so sure. I wanted them to blow me away and I came away a bit disappointed, although they did a great version of 'Celluloid Heroes' – a fabulous song. Ray doesn't get enough credit for his genius.

GOIN' DOWN DE MONT: A PEOPLE'S HISTORY

GENESIS
18 OCTOBER 1973

BRUCE PEGG

I don't remember why I ended up going as I bought a ticket without having heard the band. But something about them – maybe the cover of the *Genesis Live* album, with Peter Gabriel wearing a cape and some strange box contraption on his head – intrigued me. At any rate, I had an inkling that this show was going to be something special, so I remember buying tickets for the balcony rather than the stalls so I could soak it all in.

I wasn't disappointed. Within seconds of Tony Banks' eerie mellotron introduction to 'Watcher of the Skies', I was spellbound, despite the best efforts of a fellow audience member who thought it would be a good idea to try and break the mood by throwing a toilet roll, football-hooligan style, into the crowd below. And when Peter Gabriel finally arrived on stage, bat wings strapped to his head and his luminous eye makeup piercing through the dim, black-lit stage, I was on the edge of my seat wondering where this journey was going to take me.

For the next ninety minutes, it took me to another world, inhabited by Britannia, lawnmowers, murder victims coming back to haunt their killers, Victorian explorers and modern-day London gangsters. And just when I thought the show couldn't get any better, Gabriel told a silly story about worms writhing on wet grass and the 12-string introduction to 'Supper's Ready' began.

Seeing and hearing that piece of music unfold for the first time was overwhelming, visually and musically. Out front there was Gabriel, transforming himself into a flower ('A flower?') then Magog with that ridiculous box on his head before the final quick change out of his black catsuit into a silver lamé suit during a blinding magnesium flash. Behind him, the song twisted and turned through pastoral melodies and singsong silliness before arriving at the heavy 'Apocalypse in 9/8' crescendo and ending with its transcendent coda. Never, before or since, have my loves for literature, music, theatre, mythology and spirituality been synthesised like this into one sublime moment in time.

I went on to see Genesis five more times, including twice more at the

De Mont (21 January 1977 and 15 April 1980), but that 1973 show will always remain, with the Bowie show a few months earlier, as the two greatest musical highlights of my life.

ROXY MUSIC & LEO SAYER
30 OCTOBER 1973

CARL LIQUORISH

Back then, the De Mont was on the regular circuit for bands on tour along with places like the Manchester Free Trade Hall. Everyone came here, and the hall was always generally full. There were familiar faces in the crowd depending on your poison. Rock, metal, prog – they were all available. These days it's all about big shows: big screens, big audience numbers. Stadium rock. Corporate entertainment for those who can afford it and not necessarily in a town near you. It was a very different era back then. The shows were more intimate, the artists closer to the audience and more accessible. More affordable. More fun (or perhaps that was just our age).

We all have our specific memories. In those days, smoking and drinking was permitted in the hall. The smell of patchouli oil was always strong and there was always a whiff of weed in the air. The audience in the stalls were always standing close together. There was rarely any trouble. We were too busy enjoying the moment (no mobile phones) and all there for the same reasons. Our tribe.

My first ever gig was Roxy Music on the *For Your Pleasure* tour. The band line up included Brian Eno. I was 14 years old and sitting in the balcony. There were two support acts. A bloke called Lloyd Watson was on first. Just him, his big afro and his guitar. He sang blues, a genre I didn't appreciate at the time. He was probably good; I couldn't say. After a short break, a band came on with a singer dressed as, and fully made up as, a clown. Ladies and gentlemen, Leo Sayer. It really wasn't my cup of tea but was fairly entertaining. So far the evening was a bit of a letdown to be honest.

After a break, the atmosphere started to build to the main event. The house lights went off. Shadowy figures moved into place on stage. The crowd noise was building, as it does, but this was new to me.

Then it happened. 'Do The Strand'.

The music kicked in, fully synchronised with the lights. My jaw dropped. For the next ninety minutes or so my senses were assaulted with brilliance, but that opening line was when I fell in love with live music. 'There's a new sensation'.

NICOLA WARD
Myself and my friend Naomi went to see the *For Your Pleasure* album tour. We lived in Market Bosworth and relied on our parents to pick us up after any gigs as there were no late buses.

This was the height of the glam rock era and we were just 13, but we had to have the full make up and outfits. We would scour secondhand stalls on Leicester Market for beautiful clothes from the 1920s and '30s to get dressed up in and we'd top the outfit off with a pill box hat.

Roxy Music blew us away. It was such a wonderful concert and we wanted desperately to meet the band and hang around back stage, but my dad picked us up and whisked us away.

However we found out that they were playing in Bristol a few weeks later, and my grandparents lived there. We got our tickets and hung around the backstage doors, met the roadies, watched the sound check and were promised access to back stage after the concert.

The band (mainly Bryan Ferry) were astounded that we had travelled down all the way to Bristol to see them after watching them at the De Montfort Hall. We got taken out to dinner with the whole band, including Brian Eno who was wonderful at reassuring my panicked grandfather that we were in safe hands, and gave him the address of the restaurant where my mum could pick us up from. We stayed out until 3am. My mum joined us about 1am and had a drink with Bryan Ferry, who she rather liked. I had an old fashioned camera but no flash so the two Brians told us to pop by the hotel the next morning to get some pics.

YES
26 NOVEMBER 1973

JOANNE WHEARITY
This was my first real concert; I was aged 15. We didn't have tickets, so we climbed in through the ladies' toilets window up the side of the

building. We saw the whole show – I think it was *Tales from Topographic Oceans* – sitting on the stairs inside. Fantastic. Those were the days when the De Mont had class acts.

MOTT THE HOOPLE
22 MARCH 1974

JOHN CHAPMAN

I remember climbing up the wall next to the bar (when there was one main bar on the left side facing the stage). We shimmied along the skylight looking down into the bar, backs against the wall, up onto the lower roof, right around the front of the hall to the other side, up a bit higher and either through the girls' toilet window or a round skylight, dropping down into the stairwell going up to the back of the gallery!

MUD
21 APRIL 1974

GLENN WILLIAMS

I went with Paul Watson, one of my classmates from the City Boys, to this show. I think it was Paul's first gig and definitely only my second. Mud were on a roll, having had a recent number 1 with 'Tiger Feet' and with their new single, 'The Cat Crept In', getting heavy airplay. The support act was an eight-piece soul group called Sweet Sensation who were then unknown but were number 1 in the UK in September with their hit 'Sad Sweet Dreamer', after which they disappeared. I

Photo – John Langham

remember them being well dressed and putting on a very good, choreographed stage show. In later years, I discovered that they were being guided by Tony Hatch, who not only produced that record and sang on it but also got his wife, Jackie Trent, to add vocals to it.

I don't remember Mud's set being long – probably an hour – but I do remember they opened with 'Honky Tonk Women' and looked resplendent in sky-blue suits. The first half was all 1960s covers: 'Twisting the Night Away', 'Do You Love Me?' and others, along with a very impressive a capella version of 'Blue Moon', which would eventually surface on their first album later that year. The hits were all saved for the end, 'The Cat Crept In' being the encore.

My favourite moment was when singer Les Gray left the stage and the remaining three did a rock and roll version of Glenn Miller's 'In the Mood'. When Les returned to the stage, he was dressed like Elvis. Bassist Ray Stiles stepped up to the mic and asked the audience if they had heard of Elvis the Pelvis. A massive roar went up, after which Ray quipped, 'Well this is his brother… Enis.'

JANE RUMSEY

The De Mont was an awesome venue, although I remember playing the flute on stage there with the Leicester City Youth Orchestra, which was so embarrassing and uncool as I wanted to be 'edgy' and 'happening', God help me! Mud had 'Tiger Feet' at number one, and at the end of the concert this girl ran naked across the stage, which we now know is called 'streaking'.

SHOWADDYWADDY
25 JUNE 1974

DAVE BARTRAM, SHOWADDYWADDY

For a bunch of predominantly Leicester lads constantly travelling the length and breadth of the United Kingdom, our not infrequent visits to the De Mont often proved to be the highlight of the touring calendar, made all the more special by the knowledge that countless family and friends (who often forked out for their own tickets) would be in attendance to run the rule over the progress of their more celebrated kith and kin.

Of the many times the band visited the theatre there were many high points, beginning with our debut performance in 1974, when – somewhat apprehensively – we ventured onto the hallowed boards not quite knowing what to expect, only to leave the stage in something of a dream amidst the clamour of the crowd's rapturous reception.

BRUCE PEGG

My endearing memory of this show is of getting there. A few of us pupils at the City Boys had bought tickets to the show only to find out it was on the same night as the school prize giving. A week or so before the show, we met with our headmaster, Mr Bell, and begged him to let us out of the evening. But he ignored our pleas, even when we told him that we would be out the price of the tickets. In no uncertain terms, he told us that our attendance at the school that night was mandatory. In those days, if a headmaster told you to do something, you did it or you suffered dire consequences. We had no choice, or so it seemed.

Then, Rog Mortimer pleaded with his mother to drive us to the De Mont as soon as the evening ended, which she agreed to do. So, as soon as the last note of the school song was over, we flew out of the assembly hall, ripped off our blazers and ties, and piled into the waiting car like bank robbers leaving the scene of the crime. Off she sped, down Whitehall Road, up Evington Road, breaking every speed limit on the way. Finally, she dropped us off on Granville Road, and we sprinted into the Hall just in time to see Showaddwaddy take the stage. We may have missed the support band, and we were still wearing part of our very uncool school uniform, but at least we were able to join the sweating throng and scream for our hometown stars.

GOIN' DOWN DE MONT: A PEOPLE'S HISTORY

URIAH HEEP
29 OCTOBER 1974

STEPHEN HILL

The whole industry was in its infancy in those days – you were just getting into the big PA rigs, the big lighting rigs, visual effects, even pyrotechnics. And a lot of people made a lot of mistakes. Uriah Heep had these dry ice machines – frozen CO_2 in great big buckets like a kettle. They'd plunge it down into boiling water, and these massive clouds of white smoke would just engulf the bottom of the stage. And of course, it went into the audience, and I remember being at the gig and passing out because there was no oxygen.

CARL LIQUORISH

I remember being right at the front, leaning on the stage. The band came onto the stage and started playing. The dry ice machines were on and the smoke was drifting across the stage. A great atmosphere. But either someone messed up or a faulty machine meant the dry ice became a thick fog. Those of us at the front couldn't see their own hands in front of their faces for a few minutes. That sort of thing doesn't stop anyone having a good time. It just adds to the fun.

BRUCE PEGG

We had to evacuate our great vantage point at the front of the stage when that happened, and I remember David Byron, the band's lead singer, apologising after the first number for overdoing the dry ice. But the craziness was just beginning. The show was the last night of the *Wonderworld* tour, and I think everyone on stage was pretty drunk. I know Byron himself downed a whole bottle of Mateus Rosé during the show. For the encore, drummer Lee Kerslake ran on stage with a fire extinguisher and sprayed down his entire drum kit.

   The warm-up that night was Peter Frampton, two years before the release of *Frampton Comes Alive!* I had no idea who he was at the time, but I remember thinking that talk box was pretty cool.

GOLDEN EARRING & LYRNYD SKYNYRD
26 NOVEMBER 1974

PHIL CROUCH

At the time, we thought the show was Earring supporting Skynyrd, but I have since found out it was a 50-50 promotional tour, where both acts alternated the headline spot. Myself, Steve Hickingbottom and Keith Deacon went, and we all thought that Skynyrd were by far the better band as they played boogie blues, which was more my style of music. The standout moments were hearing 'Sweet Home Alabama' and Gary Rossington breaking a string in the main solo on 'Freebird' and just carrying on regardless.

The finale of Earring's set was a massive explosion. The drummer leapt over his drum kit, and we all thought a bomb had gone off, as it was the time of the Birmingham pub bombings. Safe to say, it's a gig that will certainly stay in the grey matter for a long time.

SUPERTRAMP
27 JANUARY 1975

PETER BURKE

Amongst many bands I worked with, I roadied for Supertramp. When they played 'Asylum', every night one of the road crew would dress up in the gorilla suit and go on stage and do their thing. My colleague Bob Harvey would usually be the gorilla, so it was always a great thrill when he would come up to me before the show and say, 'Hey Pete, do you want to be the gorilla tonight?' Prancing about on stage in a gorilla suit was great fun. I did it a few times, and I can't remember all the shows I did it, but I definitely remember doing so at De Montfort Hall.

10CC
23 MARCH 1975

CARL LIQUORISH
This was the original and best line up: Godley, Creme, Stewart and Gould. Brilliant musicians with a sense of humour. A great gig. I remember between songs opera music was played over the speakers. The band being who they were, they launched into an operatic improvisation on the spot.

THE SENSATIONAL ALEX HARVEY BAND
20 MAY 1975

CARL LIQUORISH
Alex Harvey was a great showman – one of the few front men around who had complete control over his audience. I remember him walking onto the stage to start the gig. The audience went berserk. Alex put his finger to his lips and the audience fell truly silent. He said something along the lines of, 'Good evening boys and girls. Thanks for coming to see our show. We hope you have a great time.' The band were all on stage and he says, 'This is my band. The Sensational Alex Harvey Band,' and suddenly those first repetitive notes of the 'Faith Healer' kicked in. Party time.

DUANE EDDY
24 JULY 1975

JOHN STRETTON
A gig at the De Mont had not been arranged for Duane Eddy during his 1975 UK tour, so the great man asked promoter Danny O'Donovan to slot one in so I would not miss out! The audience numbers were disappointing, but Duane, ever the showman, gave a knockout performance. The local *Leicester Mercury* reporter summed it up: 'Duane Eddy blew up a volcanic eruption last night, but where were you?' We

Duane Eddy (second left) with (left to right) John Stretton, John's wife Judi and Eddie Pumer (Capital Radio)

consoled ourselves backstage afterwards before he had to leave. Three months later, my wife Judi and I spent three weeks with Duane and his wife Deed in Los Angeles.

DR FEELGOOD
15 OCTOBER 1975

BRUCE PEGG

Most bands when they played the De Mont used to put up some kind of curtain at the back of the stage to stop the view of the choir steps and organ behind them distracting the audience from the show. On this night, the Feelgoods played their particular brand of supercharged American R&B pub rock on a very bare stage – no backdrop, just amps and drums and minimalist lighting. This was just the vehicle for guitarist Wilko Johnson to put on an even more manic performance than usual. At various points during the show, Wilko would take off on a demented run across the stage, looking for all the world like a crazed, possessed robot having some kind of seizure. But with no obstacles to stop him, at the De Mont he kept taking off up the choir steps. Wireless technology was still a few years away, so only his guitar lead stopped him from making it all the way up to the organ pipes.

GOIN' DOWN DE MONT: A PEOPLE'S HISTORY

MELANIE
17 OCTOBER 1975

JOHN CHAPMAN

Melanie was delayed by about an hour because of a late flight so did a song requests evening. The crowd called out the songs, and she played them. She wouldn't leave the stage at the required time but just carried on playing, even when they turned up the house lights and eventually turned off the PA system. She did a few more songs just on the power of her guitar and voice before finally bowing to pressure from management and finishing the show. A fantastic night, and she definitely gave value for money!

NEIL HARRIS

I had always been a great admirer of Melanie but thought it unlikely I would ever get the chance to attend one of her concerts in the UK. The opportunity unexpectedly arose to see her at De Montfort Hall. It was one of the strangest concerts I have ever attended – and probably one of the most enjoyable. I was surprised that the audience for the event was not bigger than it was. Sadly, as the evening progressed, the audience numbers diminished further as it appeared that we had a likely 'no-show' on our hands.

There was none of the usual pre-concert hype here. She eventually emerged hurriedly on to the stage very late in the evening, almost unannounced and looking a little flustered. The only thing missing was a bag of duty free. I don't recall how late she was but, as noted earlier, it was sufficient for some of the audience to have legged it into the night air and pubs.

Thankfully, setting up the stage for Melanie was not a huge job. She apologised profusely many times over for the delayed concert. She had flown in that day from Dublin and was driven straight to the venue. I think it's fair to say from her comments that she was never likely to apply for an Aer Lingus Frequent Flyer card.

She felt she had let her audience down and virtually turned the concert over to them. She gave a great performance of all her repertoire. We had comments from the floor, all laughed away, and multiple requests from the floor for songs which were all met. A very relaxed and happy atmosphere. Like all the best parties, it was one that had not been planned.

Even at the time, I realised this was something special and was certainly better than what a routine concert would have been.

The concert went on a long time. I'm not sure if there was an encore as such as she seemed to take up squatters' rights in the middle of the stage and was reluctant to move until the audience was happy. Eventually, the De Montfort Hall managed to get her to leave the stage… very reluctantly.

I'm sure this must have been one of her longest concerts, and it was great to see an artist have such respect for an audience that she felt she had let down and give the show everything. I'd love to have a recording of the concert.

URIAH HEEP
3 DECEMBER 1975

CARL LIQUORISH
After the second Uriah Heep gig I went to, we were exiting the hall and making our way through the car park and hall grounds past the tour buses and trucks. We spotted Uriah Heep's drummer, Lee Kerslake. As we were walking by him, he asked if we'd enjoyed the gig. This turned into a good half an hour of chatting and sharing a cigarette. This was someone we all saw as a rock star, but here he was chatting with us like old mates. The man was very down to earth and was about as far from the idea of a rock star as you could get. He was a top bloke.

DIANA ROSS
16 MARCH 1976

LINDA WRIGHT
I remember she had just made the film *Mahogany*, and she was wearing a white dress. Two men pulled the sleeves across the stage and they played a clip from the film on them. It was amazing.

LEONARD COHEN
13 MAY 1976

JOHN STRETTON

I was again backstage at the De Mont, this time to be one of three journalists especially invited to interview Leonard Cohen. Having reached the man in his dressing room, past his minders, the interview ended up with me taking the lion's share, as one of the other two had interviewed him a month earlier, and the other one knew nothing about him! I was told afterwards by a CBS official that it was one of the best interviews they had heard with him. I still have the tape of the conversation!

THE SENSATIONAL ALEX HARVEY BAND
22 MAY 1976

BRUCE PEGG

I'd seen SAHB the year before and was just blown away. This time, though, I don't recall if we were broke or if the show sold out before we got paid from our paper rounds, but for some reason we didn't have tickets. But we were bound and determined to get into the De Mont that night.

Stephen Hill and I hatched a plan that we would try to intercept the road crew when they arrived that morning for the show and see if we could work our way in. When the crew eventually arrived, the first person we happened across was Tam, the band's road manager. We asked him if we could help out so we could see the show, and he looked us up and down and, in a Glaswegian accent you could cut with a knife, asked us if we had jammy fingers. Being totally naive, Steve and I extended our hands and looked at them. He started laughing and hired us on the spot.

I think we humped some gear onto the stage for a while, and then I remember one of the road crew asked me if I knew where the Centre Hotel was and where there was a DIY store. I said I did, so he and I jumped in a van and I directed him first to Wilko's on Charles Street where he bought some paint and brushes. Then we went off to the hotel, and he went up to Alex's room. Sadly, I was not deemed important enough to bring along, and I had to wait in the van.

Then it was back to the De Mont, and Steve and I were put to work with the paint. Our job was to make a door-size piece of polystyrene look like a piece of brick wall. It was to be placed in a large piece of equally wall-like stage scenery behind the band, and Alex was supposed to burst through it like he had actually walked through a wall at the end of the show.

While we were painting, the band minus Alex soundchecked with 'Tomahawk Kid', and I will never forget the shock of seeing Zal Cleminson for the first time without his make up – back in those days, he appeared on stage as a white-faced clown – and thinking, 'So THAT'S why he wears greasepaint!'

The reward for our labours was being allowed to sit on the side of the stage for the show. I will never forget how cool I felt looking out at the crowd and seeing our friends out there, looking at us puzzled and wondering how the hell we were allowed on the stage.

Alex was mesmerising onstage, playing different roles – a schoolteacher reading from an oversized copy of *Treasure Island* for 'Tomahawk Kid', a crazed philosopher and comic-book character in 'Vambo', a street thug in 'Framed' – just the coolest person you could imagine. As if that wasn't enough, he was joined stage left by Zal, now in make up and blasting crunching riffs from his Gibson SG, while stage right was Chris Glen on bass, pouting and preening in a royal blue jumpsuit and codpiece, every inch the Seventies rock star.

Later, when the band broke into the double-time section of 'Give My Compliments to the Chef', I looked out at the crowd again and they were bouncing up and down with such force that I thought the floor was going to give way. But the best moment of the night for us was during 'Framed', when Alex sprayed 'Vambo Rool' on the wall before going behind it and bursting through the Styrofoam section dressed as Hitler. Our handiwork was destroyed, but the audience's evident delight made it all worthwhile.

STEPHEN HILL

I distinctly remember the part of the show when Alex Harvey kicked his way through a brick wall doing an impression of Adolf Hitler. The wall in question was actually polystyrene that had been painted black with white lines drawn to represent brickwork. A Scottish roadie had us paint the thing. I was incredibly surprised as I had never held a paintbrush in my life, but I took great care to make sure the white lines were straight. When the show came on later, I was incredibly proud that our handiwork was being kicked in by one of the biggest stars at the time!

CURVED AIR
1 JULY 1976

STEPHEN HILL

I remember being presented with a spotlight and having to stand on a flight case and point this great big white light at Sonja Kristina. I had no idea what I was doing, and I asked the guy that told me to do it, 'What do you expect me to do?' He just said, 'Point the light. If she moves, you move!' So there I was, 15 years old, standing on a flight case higher than everybody else in the middle of the audience, and I was part of the road crew. I could not have been happier. The stage was set for the next 30 years of my life.

RAINBOW
1 SEPTEMBER 1976

PAUL CANNY

Rainbow brought a state-of-the-art stage show – a 30-foot electronic rainbow spanning the stage. Groundbreaking stuff. I remember Ronnie James Dio running on to a hero's welcome even though nobody really knew him from Adam.

Ritchie Blackmore of Rainbow

BRUCE PEGG

Elaborate stage shows were still in their infancy in the Seventies, but the Rainbow show was very much a game changer and a sign of things to come. Midway through the show, Ronnie introduced the rainbow and waved his hand in a large semicircle as the lights above him followed along. And Cozy Powell performed an incredible drum solo to part of Tchaikovsky's *1812 Overture*. An amazing evening.

ALISTAIR GUYATT

I remember the rainbow rig across the front of the stage. But my main memory, as a drummer, is the solo that Cozy Powell performed. At one point he did a rim shot on his snare drum which launched a stick high into the air. He carried on playing with two feet and one stick, and when the flying stick came down he seemed to pick it out of the air without looking and carry on with both sticks. I remember it so vividly because I've never seen anything like it before or since! They were probably one of the best hard rock line ups ever – an incredible outfit.

PHIL CROUCH

During the encore, Ritchie Blackmore smashed his guitar up and threw the fretboard minus the headstock out into the crowd. And I caught it! Then, what seem like the whole of the De Mont crowd descended on me to try and rip it from my grasp. But I kept hold of it and lived to tell the tale. Another moment in a gig I will never forget.

BE BOP DELUXE
28 SEPTEMBER 1976

GLENN WILLIAMS

The conversation at school with my friend Andy 'Man' Haley went something like this:

Man: 'Going down De Mont tonight?'
Me: 'Nah. Haven't gorra ticket.'
Man: 'Neither have we. Come to my house about seven o'clock.'

GOIN' DOWN DE MONT: A PEOPLE'S HISTORY

Man lived just a 15-minute stroll from the De Montfort Hall, and walking up his street around 7pm, I noticed a half a dozen familiar faces outside his house from our school including Mick, a local lad who I knew by sight. My mother had told me to stay away from 'that Mick' on several occasions, due to his having a bit of a reputation in our area, if you know what I mean. A couple of others arrived, and we set off for the De Mont, me still none the wiser.

Once there, we hid around the corner from the right-hand fire escape doors until the main crowd had gone inside and we could hear the support band start their opening number. It was then that Mick removed a well-worn coat hanger from under his jacket and, with great stealth, crept around the front to go to work.

Back then, the fire doors were set back from the main entrance. Made of wood, the years had taken their toll on them, and there was a small gap between them through which Mick eased the coat hanger, gently bent the hanger to the left and then hooked the part inside over the crash bar and pulled back. The door swung open and Mick in a hushed voice shouted 'Go!'

We rushed around the corner. Mick was holding the door open, and I was shoved inside. The doors led to a set of stairs which I half stumbled up, not having a clue what I was doing or where I was going. Rounding the top, I found myself entering the balcony. I stopped dead in my tracks at the realisation of what had just happened, but then a smack on my back and a voice saying 'Move!' snapped me out of it. Gathering at the rear, we split up into ones and twos so as to avoid attention and made our way innocuously down the stairs into the general admission area, rendezvousing as previously arranged at the mixing desk.

'Act cool', shouted Man in my ear over the volume of the support band (who I later discovered were called Burlesque) and I did my best, but the adrenalin was still pumping. Had we really just got in to see Be Bop Deluxe for free? Yes, we had. Wow!

I learned at school the next day that this had been going on for some time with the older lads, and for the next year or so we used the technique often, but eventually the De Mont security got wise to the trick and placed guards at the top of the stairs. Undeterred, we found other ways to get in free. It was that or go back to buying tickets. What can a poor boy do?

Years later I met Harvey Goldsmith, the concert promoter that night, and the loss of revenue hadn't seemed to cause him any great financial discomfort.

THIN LIZZY
25 OCTOBER 1976

CARL LIQUORISH

It was packed in the stalls. Hot and sweaty. Lizzy were well into their set. I remember a guy a few yards in front of us. He was big and was whirling his coat above his head. A bit of an arsehole. He was asked politely by a few of us to stop. He didn't. Things started to get a bit testy. Lots of pushing and shoving, but he persisted in being obnoxious.

Suddenly, there was a tap on my shoulder. I turned. There stood a chap about eight feet tall. He gestured for me to move. I sensibly did. He tapped the obnoxious guy on the shoulder. He turned and was treated to a full headbutt which sparked him clean out. The big guy just smiled to us all and literally disappeared like smoke. The only trouble I can ever recall seeing, but sort of funny and definitely memorable. The funny thing is, everything went on like normal after that and I can't even remember the guy getting off the floor and leaving. Life's too short. He's probably a local councillor or banker now

Clover were the support act. They were decent, and one of those rare things: a support act people actually stayed in the main hall and listened to.

I saw them another time as a support act. The third time I saw them was at the NEC Arena in Birmingham. They'd changed their name by then and were massive in their own right – Huey Lewis and the News.

MARK SMIGGY SMITH, AGE 17

I drove Phil Rachael, Steve Chesterton, Chris Barlow and myself to De Montfort Hall, Leicester, my first concert. This is what I wrote in my diary afterwards:

What a concert, the first I'd been to, and I bet it'll be the best. The first group were not bad, (Clover), but not brilliant. But when Lizzy came on it was amazing. The music was loud, my god was it loud. They opened with 'Jailbreak' and then went into 'Massacre'. Fucking hell, we just went wild. I've never been so happy. I just didn't care about anyone or anything, just the music. It was the most exhilarating thing ever. The music, backed up by the lights, was just amazing. The heat was tremendous, but you didn't worry about it, you don't when you're in the middle of two thousand writhing bodies, swayed around the hall by the music. Brian Downey's drum solo was magic. Scott Gorham and Brian Robertson's guitars were completely amazing, and Phil Lynott was like a god, with everyone following him. Phil got everyone singing, stomping and freaking about. We stood at the front, right next to the speakers and they nearly blew my head to bits. Phil's guitar was soaked in his own sweat and the band really took off. They loved us and we loved them. They played 'Jailbreak', 'Massacre', 'Boys are Back in Town', 'Johnny', 'Fool's Gold', 'Borderline', 'Still in Love with You' and 'Emerald'. (The one we all sang along to was 'Baby Drives Me Crazy').

Some I didn't know. The speed of the music was terrifying. My whole body ached and sweated, the only thing that stopped me from collapsing in a heap was the sheer intensity of the music. Intense is the right word, it was as if you could reach out, take the sound, and squeeze it. Phil (Rachael) said he could see the steam rising off me. I was soaked to the skin in sweat, my clothes were smelly and wringing wet. Breathing was virtually impossible and like sweaty fire. The atmosphere was amazing, nothing can compare with the early part of this night. Nine to ten thirty. Three encores.

The atmosphere at De Mont almost tore the building down. My words, now or then, could never do it justice, as much as I have tried. It was if the earth tipped on its axis. I can still conjure up everything about that '76 night in my head – the sights, the sounds, even the smell. The 'greasers' that we ended up dancing with in the mosh pit, the chaos and pandemonium. It was anarchic. When it came to the encore the crowd was split fifty – fifty between 'Whiskey in the Jar' or 'Emerald'. The timeline at that point contained us newbies to Lizzy and also those that knew all the old stuff. At that point I hadn't heard 'Rocker', so was calling for 'Whiskey'. I didn't really know why I was shouting, because I didn't know how any of this worked. Phil played us all magically and the band stepped up with a blistering rendition of 'The Rocker'. Cue more mayhem.

GENESIS
21 JANUARY 1977

BRUCE PEGG
For their *Wind and Wuthering* tour, Genesis' light show featured 48 Boeing 747 landing lights that they hung in front of and behind the band, high above the stage. When they turned them all on during 'Afterglow' at the end of the show, and blew smoke from a fog machine onto the stage to intensify the light beams, it looked like they were playing in a giant cage. By today's standards, this is pretty tame stuff, but at the time, we were awestruck.

The other thing I remember vividly about this show is that everyone in the stalls remained seated and rapt in attention during the whole evening, even though downstairs was general admission as usual. This was the era of punk – of fans pogoing, slamming into each other, and spitting at the band – but you certainly wouldn't have known that on the evidence of this night.

GLENN WILLIAMS
That was the first time I saw a laser at a concert. The smoke drifting through gave an astonishing effect.

PAUL CANNY
This was the first of the unforgettable two-shows-in-one-day stint by the newly depleted Genesis, complete with malfunctioning inflatable monster flowers during 'Supper's Ready' and the even more monster drum kits for Phil and Chester Thompson.

LYNYRD SKYNYRD
14 FEBRUARY 1977

PAUL CANNY
You were allowed to smoke back then, and I remember the air at the gig being so thick with wacky baccy smoke that everyone was slightly high whether they smoked or not.

CARL LIQUORISH

Just a great gig. They were one of the biggest bands in the world. It was all there – the swagger, the confederate flag. Southern rock. A gig to talk about long afterwards. Then their plane crashed. We realised we wouldn't get the chance again, and were lucky to have shared the moment with them. An incredibly sad time.

BRUCE PEGG

They bought a young kid on stage to wave a Confederate flag during 'Freebird'. Then a huge area to the right of the stage cleared out during the long guitar passage at the end as people danced like crazy. It's hard to believe that eight months later Ronnie, Steve and Cassie would all die in that plane crash.

ERIC CLAPTON
20 APRIL 1977

ANONYMOUS

It was his comeback tour as he hadn't been seen for a while. A mate of mine worked for Roger Clark office equipment, and they provided the paper for the printers who printed the tickets for the De Mont. The tickets were usually on coloured paper, but for this concert they were on white paper. At the same time, Roger Clark's had a new super-duper Ricoh photo copier that was high quality.

My mate got a hold of a ticket from somewhere and proceeded to make around 50 photocopies using the same paper as the originals were printed on. He then carefully cut them out and added the little perforations down the middle and handed them out to friends. We all decided it was worth a go, as the worst that could happen was that we would be turned away at the door.

On the night, a friend and I attempted to get in, and the guy on the door said to his mate, 'Here's some more', then told us we couldn't come in and asked where we go the tickets from. We told him we had bought them off some guy outside. He said if we could point him out he would let us in.

We went outside with him and said we couldn't see the guy. He asked us to describe him, and we said, 'Long hair and in a duffle coat', which narrowed it down to about 200 people outside!

Anyway, he decided to let us in, and we joined up with others towards the rear of the hall. The De Mont had long ago removed the seats for rock concerts after the David Bowie gig, when everyone climbed all over them to get to the front.

As far as I remember, everyone who tried to get in got in. And the story made the *Leicester Mercury*!

THE CLASH
28 MAY 1977

GLENN WILLIAMS

Lance 'Butch' Clark was the kid in our year who was in the know about punk. He read the *NME* front to back every week and was the first to start wearing safety pins and ripped clothes. He looked like a punk as well. We were never mates, but then punk rock came along and we both saw the Pistols on the *Today* show in December 1976. I went to him for all my punk news as I was still more into heavy and prog rock at the time, and it was him who told me the Sex Pistols were going to play at Leicester University one Friday night. It never happened, so the first concert by a real punk band was to be The Clash at De Mont. I was going, so was Butch, and Andy 'Man' Haley and Andy Merriman as well. Both were also big Pistols fans.

We got to the De Mont in the afternoon and hung around the backstage door. Butch was messed up and dressed down and looked the part, something that could not be said for the other three of us. After an hour, a coach arrived and off stepped some punkish-looking people who we took to be the support bands (Buzzcocks and Subway Sect) followed by a few – it has to be said – rather uncouth looking women who later turned out to be the opening band, The Slits. They were followed by Joe Strummer, Topper Headon, Paul Simonon and Mick Jones, the latter of which belched at us with a grin.

Andy Merriman suggested that Butch actually looked like one of the band, and Andy Haley then urged him to follow the band in, which Butch did. The stage door closed behind him. We were quite stunned and expected the doors to open any minute and for Butch to come flying out, but he didn't.

The three of us remaining bought tickets and went in. It was a great gig. Buzzcocks were probably the best and I doubt there were 300 people inside. We caught up with Butch, who told us that he hung around backstage after he got in, wondering what to do until one of the grey-haired De Mont staff asked if he was looking for something. Quick as a flash, Butch asked him where the bar was.

'Don't you know?' asked the geriatric.

"Course not. I haven't fackin' been 'ere before, 'av I!' Butch said, after which he was left alone, chatting occasionally to the band members who no doubt wondered who the hell he was. Then he slipped into the audience as the doors opened. Walking into a gig as one of the band members: sheer class, Butch.

IAN HUNTER
9 JUNE 1977

BRUCE PEGG

I loved Mott the Hoople and Ian's first solo album after he left the band, so the choice between studying for my lower-sixth finals or seeing one of my idols was fairly easy. Sadly, I was one of the few kids in Leicester that seemed to feel that way that night, as there can't have been more than 300 or so in the audience. I have no idea why the De Mont was so empty, but I do remember 'Roll Away the Stone', played as a quiet ballad on the piano rather than the full-blown rock and roll arrangement that was a hit for Mott, was incredibly moving.

A band called the Vibrators opened the show. I think that was the first time I had seen a punk band live, and I couldn't believe the phlegm flying from the audience to the stage and back again. I only stayed for a couple of their numbers before heading to the bar.

PETER GABRIEL
21 SEPTEMBER 1977

GEOFFREY PRICE

I missed out on a nice ceramic mug from Peter Gabriel's concert. I stood right at the front of the stage, to the left as you look at it, under where Peter was sitting at his piano/organ. On the night, he must have had a sore throat or something. He was drinking a warm Lemsip drink. I looked up to him as he looked straight down at me. I had the cheek to ask for a drink; he kindly passed me the warm mug and I said, 'Thank you, Peter!' But the sting in the tail for me was, the person next to me asked for a sip. Like a fool I passed them the mug then, like the mug I was, I sadly watched it disappear along the front row, out of sight.

Peter Gabriel in action in 1977

Photo - John Chapman

WISHBONE ASH
25 OCTOBER 1977

PAUL CANNY

In the pre-Ticketmaster days, tickets for the De Mont shows had no security holograms or full-colour printing. They consisted of a black, slightly impressed overprint on a pastel-coloured, squarish piece of paper that looked like a raffle ticket. Tickets for this show were printed on pure white paper, which gave every concert-goer whose dad had access to a photocopier at work every opportunity to engage in a little amateur forgery. Consequently, there must have been scores of fans with ticket number 142. I've never seen the De Mont quite so full. I'm sure the band were suitably impressed at their popularity.

BRUCE PEGG

At the time, we thought the City Council printing office had screwed up royally, but it was probably the promoter papering the house – purposely giving away large numbers of freebies in order to make the attendance for the show bigger than it would have been under normal circumstances.

I also remember white tickets being printed for Be Bop Deluxe on one of their De Montfort Hall dates around the same time, and for Deep Purple's infamous gig at the Granby Halls on 11 March 1976. The trick with these tickets was duplicating the perforations down the middle. You had to do it just right, or else they wouldn't tear cleanly and you'd arouse suspicion on the door.

THIN LIZZY
5 DECEMBER 1977

ALAN ROBERTS

When I was seven, I passed my audition to join the Linden School choir with a rendition of 'Morning Has Broken'. This gave me my first experience at the De Mont because we became part of a huge choir of kids from all over the city for a Christmas concert that included a performance of *Peter and the Wolf*, narrated by Johnny Morris.

I remember the excitement of taking our position on the stage was right next to Johnny. But it wasn't him who caught my attention – it was the massive pipe organ behind us that gave the impression of being in a church. Little was I aware that the De Mont would become that to me very soon, as I would go on to worship my heroes from the front of the stage, looking up with the organ ever present.

My first gig was Thin Lizzy in '77. When I think back, I am immediately hit by the smell of dry ice! The house lights dropped and the loudest sound I had ever heard, except for a low-lying Vulcan bomber at Stoughton Airshow, poured out upon us as the band launched into 'Soldier of Fortune'.

I remember leaning on the stage in front of Robbo, close enough to tie his shoelaces together, which I used to think I did, but I have begun to doubt my memory as he normally wore clogs on stage!

The concert was a turning point. The whole experience was so amazing but over too soon, and I couldn't drag myself away from watching the roadies pack down the gear. I eventually had to be dragged home by my friend Adam Clay.

THE TUBES
29 MAY 1978

JOHN CHAPMAN
Fee Waybill was on incredibly high platform boots, lurching around the stage, at times with a chainsaw. I seem to remember him saying that the sunglasses he wore were too dark, and he didn't see the edge of the stage and over he went. They got him back on, but he had to be helped off, waving to the crowd as he went. The band carried on for a few more songs without him to give the crowd their money's worth. All in all, a great gig. They were outrageous live.

KEVIN HEWICK
At first it seemed like part of the show. The band did the rest of the set without him with their guitarist singing. They held up Fee's platform boots and 'worshipped' them, and I seem to recall they 'injected' them with a giant hypodermic syringe!

BLACK SABBATH & VAN HALEN
31 MAY 1978

BRUCE PEGG
The talk of this night was the warm-up band, an unknown American group that had just released their first album. Most British people aren't very fond of loud, brash Yanks, and when Dave Lee Roth strutted onto the stage and screamed 'Weeee're Vaaaaaaaan Haaayyyylennnnnn!' into the mic, a whole bunch of the audience

GOIN' DOWN DE MONT: A PEOPLE'S HISTORY

around me shouted 'Fuck off!' right back and prepared to spend the next forty minutes in the bar. Then the band launched into 'On Fire' and instantly gained two thousand fans.

Ozzy Osbourne in action at De Mont in 1978

Ozzy, Tony Iommi & Geezer Butler in action

GOIN' DOWN DE MONT: A PEOPLE'S HISTORY

RENAISSANCE
22 SEPTEMBER 1978

GLENN WILLIAMS

It was a Friday. Al Roberts and I were sharing the last vestiges of summer, our last summer of freedom, as we had both left school in July and had started our first jobs at the beginning of the month. I think Clint Watts was with us, our best mate who we had dossed with all through the school holidays at Al's, listening to records, talking the days away and basically doing nothing. Clint was staying on at school. As we headed up to the De Mont, I was as excited as could be knowing that I was about to see the new love of my life, Annie Haslam, in person, singing their July Top 10 hit 'Northern Lights'. Top of Evo Road, off the bus, short walk down Granville Street and we were there.

I remember very little about the gig apart from being at the front, stage left in front of Terrence Sullivan, 'Northern Lights' and Annie's high note at the end of 'Ashes are Burning' (which affected Al so much he acquired the live album within a week), but it was after the gig, as we were leaving, which sticks with me the most.

The foyer had a display stand using the covers of their latest album, and we asked for one each which the bloke on the merchandise stand told us to take. Then, as we were quite into collecting autographs at that time, we decided to see if we could get them signed and trooped around to the backstage door. They let us in, we had a good chat to the band, Annie was gorgeous (and petite!), we got our album covers autographed and went home.

The following morning, still buzzing from it all, we headed up town on the bus again for our regular Saturday afternoons of checking every record shop in town and hanging around the Clock Tower when, lo and behold, as we got to the top of Evo Road, Al spotted Renaissance's Jon Camp in the chippy. Well, fate had decided that we must meet him again, so we jumped off the bus at the next stop, double-backed and accosted him just as he was leaving with a big package of (presumably) fish and chips under his arm.

He was obviously hungry, but we gabbled on anyway for a few

minutes and he was polite and appreciative and thanked us for coming to the show, after which we went our separate ways. All in all, it was a rather good weekend and I still have the signed album. It's framed and hangs on my wall, a lovely reminder of my youth, old friends and nights at the De Mont.

THE JAM
2 NOVEMBER 1978

TIM FILOR

I'd only seen two bands prior to this: 10cc in 1975 and the Stranglers in 1977. The Jam came on framed by a painting of a big tower block in the background. I'd heard nothing like it before and it they just blew me away. I remember the stuff from *All Mod Cons* just leaving me breathless. I hadn't purchased or heard the album prior to the gig but storming versions of 'To Be Someone' and 'Mr Clean' left a lasting impression on me.

We were standing about halfway back from the stage. People were leaping about in front of us. I was just standing there stunned by the power of the music. Some choice cuts from the *Modern World* and *In the City* albums followed, plus most of the current singles leading up to the final number 'A-Bomb in Wardour Street'. The backdrop lit up as the song crashed to the end. We screamed for more and got it, though I can't remember exactly what the encore was.

The next day I went Christmas shopping with my mum and dad to Peterborough. I rushed into Boots and got the album. It was straight on my music centre when I got home and it didn't disappoint. The only track I don't like isn't actually listed on the back of the album, and I know a lot of Jam fans love it. Even Mike Read, the DJ, used to play it a lot, so I won't harp on any further about it other than to say that the offending article is 'English Rose'.

I remember a critic in one of the music rags reckoning that this album was Weller's rewrite of *Revolver*. What I want to know is, what track did he think was the new 'Yellow Submarine'?

SHAM 69
7 NOVEMBER 1978

BILL (LAST NAME WITHHELD BY REQUEST)
There was a bunch of skinheads kicking the main door in, so a group of us (one being me) came up with an idea to plead to the steward to be let in via the emergency entrance at the side of the front bit for safety. The other lads hid round the corner, and we all rushed in. Then a mate ordered a round of drinks, gave them out and then said, 'Oh, and a whisky,' and just walked away. We hid in the audience, and I remember Jimmy Pursey bringing a fire extinguisher on stage and inside windows getting smashed. One crazy punk gig!

THE CLASH
20 NOVEMBER 1978

RICHARD HOUGHTON
The great thing about De Mont is that it's adaptable – it can be an all seater venue or it can be all standing downstairs. And, unlike arena-sized venues, if you are downstairs and standing, you don't need a big screen to see what's going on. You're part of the action, whether you're down at the front or stood at the back. Wolverhampton Civic, Leeds O2 Academy and the (sadly now burned down) Glasgow O2 Academy are similarly-sized venues that offer the same experience.

One of my favourite shows was seeing the Clash at De Mont in 1978 on their *Sort It Out* tour. I'd first seen the Clash at Aylesbury Friars in June and sat up in the balcony, intimidated by the media insistence that punks were a threat to the established order and that I'd be taking my life in my hands by going to a punk gig as stabbings were routine, etc. This was despite my having gone to see Black Sabbath, Rainbow, Thin Lizzy and Quo, whose audiences were populated by seriously threatening-looking biker dudes who looked like they would eat a safety pin bedecked punk for breakfast if necessary, without incident. Watching the Clash from the balcony at Friars was like being a kid with his nose squashed up against the sweetshop window. I wanted to be in amongst the action. So when

I got tickets to see the Clash at De Mont, I was determined to be down front.

In November 1978, they'd just released the album *Give 'Em Enough Rope* to mixed reviews, with CBS Records having appointed Sandy Pearlman (who'd produced Blue Öyster Cult) to allegedly clean up their sound. The music press were suggesting that the Clash had sold out. If that was the case, you wouldn't know if from their performance. They opened with 'Safe European Home' and the crowd was up and bouncing from the off. I wasn't a punk sporting a mohican, but a traditional rock fan with curly hair almost down to my shoulders and wearing a leather jacket that owed more to John Travolta and *Saturday Night Fever*. But I was in the mosh pit from the beginning and stayed there until the end, bouncing around with all the other idiots. No spitting by me, though.

I can't recall everything they played, but 'Tommy Gun' and 'English Civil War' from the new album got airings, as did 'White Riot', 'Clash City Rockers', 'Complete Control' and various other of their early gems. Joe Strummer was completely in command of his audience centre stage, and Mick Jones was running up and down, doing his best Keith Richards impression (not that Keith ever ran around too much). It was semi-controlled chaos from start to finish with a non-stop barrage of fast songs and an audience full of kids in their teens and early twenties who knew they were seeing a band at the peak of their powers.

I've seen 20 plus shows at De Mont over the years, including a return visit by the Clash when they were promoting *London Calling*. This was by far the most high-energy show I ever witnessed there, and even though some of the details are hazy, I remember leaving absolutely bursting with adrenaline. It's in my top ten all-time favourite concerts.

WHITESNAKE
21 NOVEMBER 1978

ALAN ROBERTS

In those days, if you didn't have money for a ticket, or the show was sold out, you tried other means to get into the hall. One way was through the upstairs bathrooms, which involved placing a chair on a wall and shimmying up a drainpipe. However, on this occasion this proved impossible as the windows had been screwed shut.

To descend, I decided to hang from the high wall and drop down onto the chair, which was itself balanced on a wall several metres below. As soon as I was in the air, I sensed doom, and sure enough, as my feet landed on the chair, it skewed off the wall and I landed horrifically on my arms and face, scraping both down the side of the wall until I landed in a heap in thick soil. I was bleeding profusely from a wound on my forehead as well as from deep grazes on both of my arms

Meanwhile, my friends all jumped safely and painlessly onto the soft soil! They carried me, dazed and confused, to the front of the venue and pleaded through the glass doors for medical help and helped me in when one of the ushers, named Bob, complied. As I was rushed to the medical room, I saw them all run past and into the heaving venue, abandoning me! After being patched up, I myself feinted at the door as I was being escorted out and sprinted past the ageing doormen through the double doors into the concert hall, triumphantly rejoining my friends at the front.

TALKING HEADS & THE NEWMATICS
26 NOVEMBER 1978

RICH BARTON

My first experience of playing at the De Mont was like a whirlwind. I had started a job at a local factory. It was when I got home about 5.30pm or 6pm when I got a call from my band's drummer, Mallet.

> Mallet: 'You fancy going down De Mont tonight?'
> Me: 'No, I'm knackered! I think I'll just watch telly.'
> Mallet: 'No, you won't! We're on at 7.30. We're supporting Talking Heads!'

Wow! What a buzz. I soon livened up, got my best threads out and made my way down.

As it turns out, we replaced the Human League, who had been kicked of the tour by the Musicians' Union for using tapes. We were going to warm up for Talking Heads at the time of *Fear of Music*. It was a big moment for us.

One memory is being shocked at hearing my own backing vocals, because we actually had monitors. We also got to hang out with Tina Weymouth and Chris Frantz after the show. She thought it was hilarious that we called cigarettes 'fags'!

Mallett went on to play with Tranvision Vamp and the Rotten Hill Gang collective. He's still my best mate.

SHOWADDYWADDY
19 DECEMBER 1978

DAVE BARTRAM
Arguably the most joyful of all our concerts. Barely two hours prior to running out on stage, we received word from our record company that our newly released *76-78 Greatest Hits* album had incredibly reached the top spot in the UK charts to bestow the band with a prestigious Christmas number one album, an achievement shared with the sell-out audience during an early break in our performance.

The ecstatic roar reached to the rafters, similar to a winning goal in a World Cup final, as moments later the band members gleefully soused the packed crowd – Grand Prix-style – with a case full of hastily purchased champagne. Needless to say, the after-show party extended way beyond the next day's dawning!

UFO & LIAR
5 FEBRUARY 1979

ROCKY NEWTON, LIONHEART
I lived in Grantham, and the closest venue for the major acts to us was the De Mont. There were no trains, so there were a couple of ways we used to get there. I was doing a business studies course at Grantham College, and for a while I was the Social Secretary there, so we would get buses, sometimes organised by me but others also did it. A form would go up, and you'd put your name down if you wanted to go and see Rush

or UFO or whoever. We'd fill the bus up and the cost would be split across everybody.

The other way of getting there was my car, which I always had. I passed my test six weeks to the day after my 17th birthday. I had been brought up on a farm and had been driving since I was about ten years old, because on a farm there are tractors and always old bangers laying around. I had a minivan and we used to cram about ten people in it and all bundle up to Leicester.

To be honest, I don't recall a lot of the actual gig as it was so long ago, and it only took on significance later. As with most support bands back then, if they didn't impress you in the first two or three numbers, you would head off to the bar. But if I remember correctly, I had Liar's *Set the World On Fire* album before I joined Lionheart, which says Liar must have impressed me at the time.

Then of course when I did join Lionheart in late 1980, fairly early on Steve Mann and I started chatting about which bands we had been in, and he mentioned he'd been in Liar, which of course was the support band at the UFO gig. So yeah, I watched Steve as a fan on the De Mont stage and then not long after joined a band with him in. And I'm still in it!

THIN LIZZY
5 APRIL 1979

COLIN WOOD
My very first gig was Lizzy at Leicester's De Mont for the *Black Rose* tour. The atmosphere was awesome. The gig was more than a sell out as many, many fans were climbing through upstairs windows to get onto the balcony. I was standing in the middle, about a third of the way back, so had a clear view of these fans. The band themselves were awesome and climaxed with Gary Moore playing 'Black Rose' as the encore.

MARK SMIGGY SMITH
My diary entry for this gig reads:
What more can I say, except that it was the best yet. Got right up to the front. Blinded and singed by magnesium flares, kicked in the head,

fookin' sweated my bollocks off. Angie came too and, although obviously not getting off on the atmosphere during the first ten to 15 minutes, she soon fell into the swing of things. I must say that this is what I like best of all. The sound and the atmosphere just carry you up and away to another dimension where you couldn't care whether you lived or not.

ROXY MUSIC & THE TOURISTS
2 MAY 1979

MARK HEALEY

I first met Glenn Williams when I was 16; we were apprentices at Marconi Radar together. Soon after, he started trying to get me to go along to a live concert. I wasn't convinced: why would seeing someone live be any better than listening to an album? I finally agreed to see Roxy Music at the De Montfort Hall.

I did have a couple of Roxy Music records but I wouldn't say that I was a fan. They were just another band at the time that I liked. As the day of the concert approached I surprisingly found myself getting excited. I felt genuine anticipation. As I said, I worked with Glenn at the time and he kept saying every day that I was in for a treat. It started rubbing off on me and I really did look forward to going.

Roxy Music 1979 UK tour programme

On the night of the concert I had to take a bus from home to the city centre then walk about a mile to the venue. I was extremely nervous, but excited: what would it be like? what if I didn't like it? what if I didn't fit in? We had agreed to meet at the Marquis Wellington on London Road. This became a familiar pattern in the future.

Joining the crowd of people entering through the large doors at the entrance of the Hall, the atmosphere of anticipation was tangible, the smell, the noise, the clothes of some of the real fans. Even the wooden floor felt different. The place seemed to vibrate with a kind of hum, I hadn't known anything like it. My parents hadn't been theatre goers when I was young, not even going to pantomimes, so it was all completely new to me. And I liked it!

So the support act started and I was transfixed. It was very loud and it was very bright! There was Annie Lennox on the stage, who was then completely unknown to us, singing with The Tourists. I was hooked. It took 30 seconds and I knew that I would want more. I'd completely forgotten who I was, it was a different world, one I wanted to be part of. I now realised what Glenn had been talking about. Of course Glenn, the old hand at this sort of thing (even at 17!) was very blasé at this point, although he did say, 'Not bad for the support!'

We were off to the bar at the interval for another pint and then quickly back to our seats. The momentum slowly began to build. Slow hand claps and periodic chants of 'We want Roxy' added to the nervous energy enveloping the Hall. Glenn remarked to me that, 'This is different, I've never seen a stage curtain before, they usually just walk on stage.' I think he was kind of excited too!

Then the Hall background music fell silent and it seemed that at the same instant the crowd momentarily went quiet too. The curtains drew back and the crowd bayed. The stage set had a kind of geometric design and was lit to highlight the modernistic look. Glenn looked at me and said 'Wow!' Bryan Ferry was singing 'Love Is the Drug', and everyone was singing along.

The next two hours seemed to fly by.

At the end Glenn said 'You're lucky. They're not all like that you know.' All I knew was that I wanted to see more. The next day I went out and bought *Reality Effect* by The Tourists and *Manifesto* by Roxy Music. I was a convert, and I never needed convincing again to go to another show.

IAN DURY & THE BLOCKHEADS
16 JULY 1979

BRUCE PEGG

As a kid, Ian was paralysed on his left side due to contracting polio. My enduring memory of this show was seeing him get into the music so much that his left leg would collapse and he would fall over, which happened several times throughout the set. At that point, a roadie who was strategically placed on the side of the stage would pick Ian up and station him back behind his mic stand without missing a beat.

The end was pretty strange, too. Instead of walking off stage at the end of the encore, the band sat on the stage riser and waved goodbye to the crowd as the house lights went up. Of course, once they realised that we thought they were going to stay for one more song, they finally got up and walked off.

2-TONE TOUR – THE SPECIALS, MADNESS, THE SELECTER & DEXY'S MIDNIGHT RUNNERS
5 NOVEMBER 1979

MARTIN PAGE

The Selecter, Madness and The Specials played (£2 ticket!). Me and my sister attended (with our own gangs), and my dad insisted on picking my sister up, her being 14 or 15, it being late and also 15 miles from home. He waited outside as the doors opened but he worked his way into De Mont. At some point he got caught up in the rush as all three bands came on stage to do 'Skinhead Jamboree', and to this day Dad maintains that he ended up on stage with the bands and 'loads of hooligans'. At 88, he still has a soft spot for ska!

GOIN' DOWN DE MONT: A PEOPLE'S HISTORY

AC/DC
9 NOVEMBER 1979

ALAN ROBERTS

I met so many of my heroes at the De Mont, but the one that stands out was Bon Scott, the AC/DC singer, when he was still alive.

I can't say it was the best gig I saw there, as Bon was too drunk to sing. But after the show ended, I was – as usual – the first to arrive backstage after the show. I was swiftly followed by a few hundred others who desperately wanted to meet the hottest band of the moment. After a 45-minute wait, the stage door opened and a burly roadie grabbed my arm and pulled me in, shutting the door swiftly behind me.

Bemused but overjoyed, I ran up the stairs to be greeted by Angus Young impersonating a charging bull and careering towards me over the landing! I then had no choice but to swirl my denim jacket as a matador would and shout 'Olé!' This surreal scene continued and I spent one of the most fantastic nights of my life in the company of Bon, Angus and the boys, leaving in the early hours of the morning clutching my souvenirs, which included a flyer for the following week's De Mont show signed by Bon with the phrase, 'Who the fuck are Blue Öyster Cunt!'

PAUL SANKEY

Angus Young did a guitar solo and walked offstage still playing. He carried on playing and then appeared next to me on a roadie's shoulders still playing. Sweat was spraying everywhere. Oh, for a mobile phone camera then!

THE DAMNED
22 NOVEMBER 1979

GLENN WILLIAMS

Dave Vanian used the trapdoor to appear onstage as they launched into the opener, 'Love Song'. They closed the show with 'Smash It Up'/'Ballroom Blitz'. The other bands on the bill that night were Victim from Belfast and the Misfits from the US. That was the only show the Misfits played on that tour and in the UK; an associate of mine was on the tour, and he told me they were kicked off because they were never officially on. It was a hell of a night!

ANTHONY SMITH

The Misfits were brilliant. It was the only UK gig they played with Glenn Danzig singing. Victim were good as well, and I remember Dave Vanian coming out the trapdoor.

There was a backstage party after the gig and a load of us got in. I remember Algy Ward hitting a young lad over the head with a bag full of badges. I also recall Rat Scabies and Captain Sensible tying a lad up with a roller towel because he had a UK Subs t-shirt on. And Sensible's suitcase was nicked, with his furry jumper and the demos for *The Black Album*, the Damned's next album, in it.

THE JAM
18 & 19 DECEMBER 1979

BRUCE PEGG

If you had long hair in the late Seventies, as I did, going to a punk or New Wave show sporting long hair in England was a risky move. I'm not exaggerating when I say that you were pretty much taking your life into your hands. But I was a huge Jam fan, and couldn't resist going, so I enlisted my friend Glenn Williams for moral support. The band were their usual incredible high-energy selves and well worth taking the chance that we might get beaten up. But to be safe, we came in late and pretty much everyone was inside. We hung right at the back of the hall where no one would see us, leaving during the encore and legging it over

Photo - Tim Filor

Victoria Park to the relative safety of the Old Horse for a quick pint before going home.

GLENN WILLIAMS
The support band that night was The Vapors, who had just been discovered by Bruce Foxton and John Weller, The Jam's bass player and frontman Paul Weller's father respectively. Two months later, they were in the charts with 'Turning Japanese'.

BLONDIE
27 DECEMBER 1979

MARK HEALEY
Alan Raymond was a work colleague for a short time in 1979. As an 11-year-old boy, he had been involved in a hit-and-run road traffic accident that meant that he had to have both his legs amputated just above the knees. When I knew him, I guess he was in his mid-thirties, and we worked together at Marconi. He used a wheelchair to get around, but mostly he would use his upper body strength to propel himself across the long work benches on his hands. His arm muscles were enormous.

I mention all this because when it became known that Blondie had included Leicester as one of their tour dates for their first ever concerts in the UK, he was very excited. We all were. Debbie Harry was an icon with stunning looks, and their music in 1979 and 1980 was probably the biggest thing at that time. We knew that the demand for tickets would outstrip the supply. So, it was Alan that suggested that he was willing to queue all night for tickets in his wheelchair. An individual could buy four tickets each and Alan offered two of them to Glenn Williams and myself.

We immediately said yes.

I never saw the queue, but the tickets were all sold on the morning they became available and all to those in that massive overnight queue that had formed. I still can't believe that Alan had been so willing to offer us the tickets; he could have sold them at many times their face value.

The concert was the day after Boxing Day 1979 and is definitely one of my all-time favourites. I took my camera but didn't manage to get one decent shot. In fact, I took one shot and then gave up. The audience was in a real party mood and didn't stop moving and dancing for the whole time. Debbie Harry was in great form, and from start to finish it was one hit after another and I wanted to join in!

MARTIN BEANE

I paid a week's wages, about £30, for a ticket to a tout outside after trying to buy one for about two hours. I ended up standing centre stage about six feet from the front. Still to this day it is one of the best nights I ever had at a gig.

JOHN DANAHER

From memory, there were signs of the discontent that would later emerge publicly. Debbie was perfectly Debbie, and some of the guys were on it, but some of them looked disinterested.

GLENN WILLIAMS

Mum and Dad had the *Mercury* delivered every night. I did no more than look to see if there were any new gigs announced and I knew every band that was coming and the date by heart, so I was a bit surprised when my mate at work, Mark Healey, said, 'Going to see Blondie?' For a while I thought he was pulling my leg, but it turned out to be true. Blondie were going to play De Mont, but for reasons unknown, it just wasn't being advertised.

Mark got the tickets. £4.25 – a bit steep but what the hell, it was Blondie, the hottest band on the planet. To think I was going to see Debbie Harry in the flesh – well, that was going to be my best Christmas present that year.

Marconi, where I worked, was closed for the Christmas break, so we had the day off. It was bitterly cold and rain was forecast, but I decided to head down to the De Mont early in the hope of catching a glimpse of the band when they arrived. I wasn't the only one with the same idea, and I was happy to see that I'd be sharing the inclement afternoon with a couple of mates, namely Ian and Phil, who were part of the local music scene with Manitou.

I think it was about 2pm when I rocked up and we waited and waited.

3pm, 4pm, 5pm… still no Blondie. It was dark, I was running out of cigarettes, and we were getting colder and wetter by the minute. 6pm. Where the hell were they?

They were late. It was the start of the tour. They had flown in from the US on December 21st, recorded *Top of the Pops* and then opened in Bournemouth on the 26th. By that time, most of the band had colds, and Debbie had it the worst. The rain was turning into a downpour.

Twenty minutes later, two large headlights cut through the night and the rain, and a big bus turned into the gates behind the De Mont. It drove round the rear garden and parked, its headlights blazing on the backstage door and us, who by now had grown into a dozen. The door opened and the band rushed past us into the venue.

Someone from their entourage was barking that they needed a chemist. I didn't fancy their chances of finding one open at 6.30pm the day after Boxing Day in Leicester, but I said nothing.

Then suddenly, there she was. Debbie, wrapped in coats and scarves, was bundled through us, clearly suffering with a bad cold but she managed a smile which was all we had hoped for. Chris Stein got off the bus and took photos of us. He told the tour manager to let us all in to see the show, and as the last of the band went in, we were ushered through the backstage doors into the auditorium.

The gig was cloud nine. They opened with 'Dreaming' and ran through their greatest hits in an hour. I got to the front, almost touching distance. I was soaking wet throughout but didn't care. The encore was The Kingsmen's 'Louie Louie' – a bit of a let-down to be honest, as I was well into Motörhead at the time, who had recently killed it in their version.

It didn't matter. 'Sunday Girl', 'Heart of Glass' and 'Hanging on the Telephone' more than made up for it.

I bought a poster and stuck it on my bedroom wall that night. The poster is long gone but the memory remains, aided by the publication of Chris Stein's book *Making Tracks*, published a couple of years later with his photo of us waiting in the rain in it. A gig I was fortunate to be at thanks to Mark. To my knowledge, it still the only gig that has sold out at the De Mont without being advertised.

Ian Rawlings was photographed by Blondie's Chris Stein

IAN RAWLINGS

It's September 1979, and I'm on my weekly pilgrimage to the newsagents to purchase a copy of *Sounds* – for me the rock music newspaper at that time. This particular week's edition announced that Blondie were touring the UK and they were playing the De Mont! Awesome news.

Not so awesome was that by the time I managed to ring the box office about tickets they had already sold out.

The gig was on December 27th, so myself and a couple of mates, Paul Fairey and Phil Whysall, decided to pop along to the De Mont early that morning to see if we could work/roadie for some tickets. Sadly we were told no, but rather than return all the way back to 'sunny' Rutland, we thought we'd hang out at the backstage door and see if we could blag entry there. Morning turned to afternoon, and the weather turned to rain, so we sheltered in the doorway. Unfortunately the doormen/security were not happy with our presence, and repeatedly tried to get us to leave with idle threats, including telling us that the grounds were now closed and they had let the dogs out!

Undeterred, and as we'd been standing there for a few hours now, we decided to wait for the band to arrive for a soundcheck, so at least we'd get to see them before we went home. We were also joined by a few more people, obviously thinking along the same lines as us, one of which was Glenn Williams. I was playing bass in the band Manitou at the time; Glenn was the roadie for Manitou and a friend of Bruce Pegg, Manitou's singer. So it was good to see him that afternoon.

By late afternoon, while the doormen were still (unsuccessfully) trying to get rid of us, a large tour bus finally appeared. The members of Blondie disembarked, surrounded by security, and made their way to the backstage door where we were huddled. As the doors opened we moved out of the way to allow them entry, and Debbie Harry passed us by within touching distance along with the rest of the band. Chris Stein stopped to chat, asked how long we'd been there, and took photos of us looking wet and bedraggled. He then followed the rest of the band into the hall and went in to soundcheck.

After the soundcheck the band went back on to the bus. Again, Chris Stein stopped to talk to us as he was surprised we were still there. He told us that if we were still there when the band returned he would get us into the gig. This resulted in two things: it made us decide to stay, despite the fact we'd been there for many hours in the cold and wet, and it upset the doormen even more!

After what seemed a long wait (and even more hassle from the backstage doormen), the tour bus finally reappeared. As the band filed past and the doors slowly closed, the doorman laughed and took great delight in telling us we wouldn't be getting in. We were obviously very disappointed and about to leave when the backstage door suddenly re-opened and Chris Stein emerged, pointed to us all and said to the doorman, 'I want you to show these guys into the hall.'

We didn't get to meet or see the band backstage but were led down a corridor and given free entry to the hall via a door to the left of the stage. We quickly went to the front of the stage and that's where we stayed for the rest of the evening. Needless to say the whole experience was worth it. Blondie were amazing and I will cherish those memories forever.

Finally, the following Christmas my parents bought me a book – *Making Tracks, the Rise of Blondie*. On reading through it, one particular page caught my eye. It featured two photos, the top one was captioned 'Fans waiting in the sun', and the bottom one was captioned 'Fans waiting in the rain', which was a photo taken of us standing outside the De Mont backstage door that cold and wet day back in December 1979.

GOIN' DOWN DE MONT: A PEOPLE'S HISTORY

THE CLASH
16 JANUARY 1980

RICH BARTON

By now The Newmatics were becoming a big local draw, so when the Clash came to town and wanted a local band to support them, we got the gig. The Clash were anti-establishment punk princesses. I sneaked a look in their dressing room. Mick Jones had five Les Pauls in a semi-circle, all ready to go, more rock star than punk. But the energy they created on stage was awesome. I had no idea what was coming out of Strummer's mouth, but it was heartfelt. They were great after the show, chatting and sharing drinks and a spliff, although Topper did seem on edge.

PETER GABRIEL
24 FEBRUARY 1980

BRUCE PEGG

It would be hard to recall another show that rivalled this one for sheer drama. Back in the day, artists would time their tours to coincide with the release of their new album, but by the time the tour began four days before this show, Gabriel's third album still hadn't appeared – rumour had it that he didn't like the first mix and had delayed the release date so he could go back into the studio and remix it. It eventually came out that May. But Gabriel insisted that the show should showcase his new material, so the audience was confronted by a number of songs that they had never heard before, interspersed with more familiar material from the first two albums.

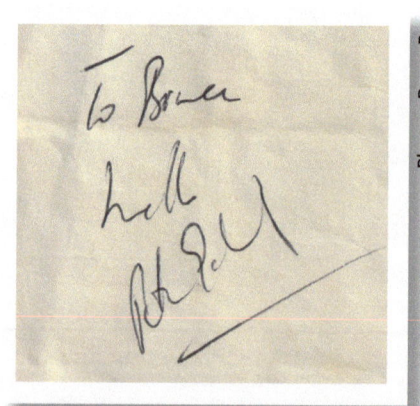

Bruce Pegg got Peter Gabriel's autograph

With the opening drum beats of 'Intruder', the house lights went down, and the band, dressed in work overalls, began to walk from the back of the hall and through the crowd toward the stage, establishing an unsettled feeling that continued for the rest of the performance. At one point in the show, Gabriel took a backward trust fall off the stage into the crowd and crowd surfed, which I'd never seen an artist do before. Then he used a wireless mic – again, the first time I can recall an artist using one – to sing, first in the balcony and then down in the stalls, where he popped up immediately behind me and shook my hand as he walked past.

But the highlight of the show came toward the end of the evening. For the last song, he took the risky move of playing 'Biko' from the yet-to-be-heard new album. Few artists I know would ever dare finish a show with an unheard song, much less a politically-charged ballad such as this. But the simple, repetitive drum pattern and chanting vocals immediately resonated with the crowd, and by the end of the song, the whole of the hall was singing along in spine-tingling fashion. Then, for the encore, rather than playing an out-and-out rocker, Gabriel walked on stage and played an incredibly moving version of 'Here Comes the Flood', sitting alone on stage at the piano, before the band rejoined him for a rousing 'On the Air'.

After the show, we waited for what seemed like an eternity for him to come out. He signed a quick autograph for me, then made his way off into the dark.

GLENN WILLIAMS

When the lights went down and the intro music started, a cheer went up and we faced the stage waiting for him to appear. Except he didn't. We stood there wondering what was happening, when someone next to me shone a bright torch in Bruce's face. Before my eyes could focus, the torch whirled around into my eyes, blinding me for a few seconds. Then it vanished and I focused. I looked at Bruce who was looking at me. Simultaneously we looked towards the source of the light and stared in disbelief at the man himself walking through the audience from the back of the hall, tapping people on the shoulder, edging his way towards the stage, his band mates doing likewise, spread out across the auditorium. Those at the front had no idea of the theatrics going on behind them: we were in awe.

At the end of the night, the stage lights faded, and there was a low bass note from the keyboards accompanied by a simple percussion rhythm and a droning guitar. A spotlight hit Gabriel full in the face and he launched into a short monologue about Steve Biko. I know nothing of the man until that moment. Throughout the song, Gabriel's face portrayed pity, anger, sympathy, sincerity and heartbreak as he sang this new anthem. He and band stood motionless for the duration of the song. There were no lighting changes other than a gradual fade of white over the stage. Bruce, myself and over two thousand other fans were left dumbstruck by the sheer power of it. We applauded almost in disbelief.

NICK MEE
There was a rather strange incident outside the stage door after the Gabriel gig. A weird guy had been hanging about, and when Gabriel came out this weird fella came up to him and told Gabriel that he was Satan and that he wouldn't hurt Peter. At this point, security got Gabriel into a Range Rover and off he sped. Quite a few people saw the incident.

SARAH MCPHERSON
I first went to the De Mont to see Mud (my first ever gig at the age of 12). I also played there several times with various school orchestras at their infamous Gala Concerts, the highlight of which for me was playing the *1812 Overture* with the mass orchestra and Richard Stilgoe, of dodgy TV fame, on cannon!

Anyway, I went with Bruce to see Peter Gabriel. We were in the stalls, and the band came on through the audience with handheld searchlights – very atmospheric. After the gig, which was great, Bruce wanted to see if he could get an autograph, so we headed round to the back of De Mont, where there are two stage doors. A load of people were waiting by the left-hand stage door, when there was a sudden dash to the right-hand stage door which had opened.

I stayed sitting on the railing by the left-hand stage door as I wasn't fussed about an autograph. The door opened and out came a pleasant young man who looked at me. I looked at him. He asked if I had enjoyed the gig. I said I had. He asked if I wanted his autograph. The only thing I had on me was my ticket stub, which he signed, and was then mobbed by everyone running back from the other stage door. Poor Mr Gabriel – being met by a young, rather underwhelmed fan as he exited after a great gig high!

RICHARD HOUGHTON
There was quite a buzz around Peter Gabriel in the music press. After all, here was someone who'd turned his back on Genesis, one of the

biggest bands of the Seventies, in pursuit of creative freedom. It's all there in the song 'Solsbury Hill'. I remember standing in the crowd waiting for the band to come on and they each emerged from the audience, Gabriel included, carrying large flashlights with them. It was quite the entrance (which, of course, had much less impact when I saw the same show a few weeks later at Hammersmith Odeon). And, after the gig, I hung around the stage door and got his autograph on my student identity card. He signed it, 'To Richard – Peter Gabriel', and it takes pride of place in my ticket collection, which hangs in a frame on the upstairs landing.

NICK FARRIN
I managed to get in on the night to see Peter Gabriel. He and his band entered a dark hall from the back and balconies wearing black jumpsuits with a white diagonal line across the front and carrying searchlights. I didn't realise at first that they were the band.

THE TOURISTS
25 FEBRUARY 1980

MARK HEALEY
One of things Glenn Williams and I would do at the end of a concert at the De Montfort Hall, as long as it finished before 10pm, was to go to the rear of the hall to the stage door. There were often a number of fans there all waiting to catch a glimpse of the stars and try and get an autograph. Mostly we would wait ten to 15 minutes and then give up. I had to get back to the bus station for 10.55pm for the last bus home, and it was a 30-minute walk. Getting a taxi home was too expensive.

So, after we had seen The Tourists perform for the first time as a headline act, we rushed back to the stage door as usual. What wasn't usual was that we were there so quickly that we ended up as first in the queue. In fact, within a few minutes there were probably around another 25 fans waiting. Something else was different, because after about five minutes someone opened the stage door and invited the first four in the queue up to the dressing room. That obviously included Glenn and myself.

In the dressing room were Annie Lennox and Dave Stewart. I don't remember seeing the other band members, but they may have been there too. Dave Stewart was sitting in a chair and plainly completely drunk. He had a glass of something in his hand and wasn't in any kind of control of his physical actions. He said 'Hi', but that was about it.

Annie Lennox of The Tourists

Annie Lennox was wearing one of those plastic fake boob breastplates over the top of her clothes, like the one later made famous by Paul Gascoigne at *Italia '90*. This was a bit of shock. It seems so innocent now but back then it really was outrageous, at least it was to me. Annie pointed to a long bench type table along the side of the wall which was full of various alcoholic drinks and said, 'Help yourself', which we both did.

Annie Lennox signed Mark's programme

Glenn was super cool, but I was entirely star struck. I couldn't string any kind of sentence together at all. A few nods of the head and 'yeses', probably at inappropriate moments, was all I could manage! Glenn asked some questions, I've no idea what they were, I think I was in shock. We duly got their autographs and after around 20 minutes we were ushered away again back down the stairs. Another truly unforgettable experience.

SAMMY HAGAR
8 APRIL 1980

BOB GILL
Having strict, first-generation immigrant parents, overly and inevitably obsessed with studies and exams, must have contributed to my concert-going being more selective than prodigious. Looking back, I must have been very conspicuous in the crowd of white faces, as I was usually the one and only Asian in attendance. But to the credit of the heavy rock/metal fraternity in those rather fraught times (rapidly rising unemployment, National Front marches, skinheads, etc.), I cannot recall experiencing any racial problems at all.

But it was not just the concerts themselves. There was the thrill of seeing the listing in the *Leicester Mercury* that of one your favourite bands was set to come to town. The queuing up at the Town Hall to get your tickets. And the anticipation of the evening ahead as you rode the 67 bus from Evington into the city.

It was not even a full house that early spring night, just after the clocks had gone forward, as Hagar, while moderately successful, was not exactly up there with the rock titans of the age – he only received wider recognition after taking the tough gig of replacing Dave Lee Roth in Van Halen a few years later. But for 17-year-old me, he was cool. I mean, he came out of Montrose, they of the brilliant and legendary eponymous debut album, and he sang about Trans Am cars, sweet hitchhikers, bad motor scooters and making it last.

'I thought this was just a small college town, but you guys can really rock!' he exclaimed as he ran back on stage for the encore of the show. The words may not be exact, diluted as they are through more than 40 years, but you get the idea.

GOIN' DOWN DE MONT: A PEOPLE'S HISTORY

GENESIS
15 APRIL 1980

PAUL CANNY
Back in the Seventies and early Eighties, tickets for the De Mont were sold from the office in Town Hall Square, and on some occasions, it was necessary to queue overnight to ensure you got a ticket, particularly if there was a limit on the number you could buy. The queue for Genesis tickets in 1980 was gatecrashed first thing the next morning and absolute bedlam ensued. The crush became dangerous – the police were called and many of us had to get out without managing to get tickets. Luckily, a friend of mine from Loughborough Art College managed to get several tickets and was able to sell me a couple, so that I did get to go in the end.

BRUCE PEGG
I was one of the lucky ones, probably one of the first 15 or 20 people at the front of the queue when the box office opened. I managed to get my allocation of four tickets and got out of there quickly as I had to get back to college for one of my classes that morning. So, I didn't see the problems that occurred after I left.

NEIL HARRIS
There was a long wait, and when the box office opened the queueing system went to hell. Folks who had just appeared charged to the front. It was really frustrating, but I managed to grab a couple of tickets. But the show was well worth the hassle.

CHRIS WIBBERLEY
When the box office opened in the morning, my then girlfriend got badly crushed in the queue and ended up at the Leicester Royal Infirmary. She was okay, but the box office staff had seen what happened and had saved us some tickets, which some friends picked up whilst we were in A&E.

MARK HEALEY
For me, the most notable thing about this concert was that I had my camera confiscated! As usual, the rear of the ticket had all the small

print clauses and regulations printed on it including that no cameras or recording equipment were allowed. This was no different to most other bands and I had taken my camera to a number of

Phil Collins of Genesis at De Mont

Photos - Mark Healey

previous concerts without any bother. I think most just accepted that there would be a few amateur photographers.

But in preparation for this concert I had bought a new zoom lens and it did stick out quite a bit. Anyway I had learnt a technique whereby I placed the camera neck strap over one shoulder. I then put my jacket on over the top to hide it. If I was frisked, I would just lift my arms up raising the camera at the same time in one swift move, so that the camera would remain hidden.

Genesis 1980 UK tour programme

Sometimes the bigger named bands would stipulate in stronger terms the camera restrictions, and Genesis was one such group to do this. But this wasn't going to put me off. Glenn Williams had queued all night for tickets (one of his favourite bands) and had got prime seats on the fifth row of the balcony and in a central position. Genesis were a huge band, and to get some photos would be amazing.

So once the house lights went down and the band appeared, I removed my coat and carefully got my camera out hoping no one would see it in the semi-darkness. At first, I was quite subtle about it and managed to shoot off a couple frames. But then as I became more confident I was taking more and more. It was only around ten minutes in when a steward spotted me and beckoned me to leave my seat and approach him. I pleaded innocent of course but he insisted that I hand the camera in at the luggage/cloakroom.

So that was that. I was little surprised that they hadn't asked me to give them the roll of film. Of around 20 shots that I managed to take, there was one that I was pleased with and it is one of my all-time favourites.

DEF LEPPARD
27 APRIL 1980

ALAN ROBERTS
I can remember being so excited to read in *Sounds* that the young band Def Leppard would be visiting our hallowed Hall and immediately secured a ticket. The concert itself, with Quartz supporting, was fantastic as seen from my regular spot leaning on the stage. The late Taffy Taylor was in fine form, exchanging banter with the crowd like a backroom pub comedian, and in fine voice too, especially on 'Satan's Serenade', while the highlight of the Lepps set for me was a new song called 'Lady Strange'.

However as the gig ended, the magnetic pull to the stage and the backstage area was too strong and I sneaked through corridors until I found the dressing room without having to queue outside the backstage door to meet the band.

Steve Clark recognised me from in front of him earlier, and we had a great chat which ended with me playing some of my riffs to him and him being so kind and genuinely interested in my band. It was one of the first times that I got to meet bands, but I would never have thought that two years later I would be on tour with Def Leppard and spending time with Steve again while working for their support band, Rock Goddess.

RICHARD HOUGHTON
I'd seen Def Leppard at Loughborough Town Hall, as Bruce Pegg was raving about them, and I'd quite enjoyed that as metal – in the shape

of Sabbath, Lizzy and UFO – was my thing really. This was a step up, venue-wise, and a sign that Leppard were in the ascendant. But I found the gig strangely antiseptic, although I was clearly in a minority as the crowd loved it. Bruce took me backstage afterwards. Lead singer Joe Elliott was sat at a piano, trying to write a song. All I could think of to say to him was 'nice light show'. It was a nice light show.

SKY
12 MAY 1980

BRUCE PEGG

Sky were a prog rock outfit formed by classical guitarist John Williams. The show itself was forgettable except for a brief moment that only the De Mont could produce. Part way through the show, Francis Monkman, their keyboard player, climbed up the choir steps at the back of the stage and played Bach's 'Toccata and Fugue' on the Hall's organ. It was the first and only time I ever heard the organ played; I don't believe the Hall ever gave permission for any rock band to play it. When he hit that ominous low chord in the introduction, the whole building shook. I know Motörhead were probably the loudest band to appear at the De Mont during this time. But even they didn't shake, rattle and roll the De Mont's foundations the way Mr Monkman did that night.

BLACK SABBATH
26 MAY 1980

RICHARD HOUGHTON

I was excited about seeing Sabbath with Ronnie James Dio. Although the idea of him replacing Ozzy took a bit of getting used to – I'd seen him fronting Richie Blackmore's Rainbow, at the Rainbow, a couple of years before – I thought *Heaven and Hell* was a decent album. Not classic Sabbath, but better than *Tech Ec*. And I was interested in seeing what sort of a fist Ronnie made of stuff like 'War Pigs' and 'Iron Man'.

I went with Bruce Pegg. I can't remember whose idea it was to get there early but it was probably his as he was a De Mont veteran, having seen Bowie, Genesis and others there, what with it being his local venue. We were right down front, which was a good idea given that neither of us are towering giants. Waiting for Sabbath to come on, we were speculating on what the stage effects and lighting were going to be. (In those days of course you didn't have YouTube to look at and TV footage of rock concerts pretty much didn't exist.) But we didn't need YouTube to spoil the surprise. We had the bloke stood next door to us, who had already seen an earlier show on the tour and who then proceeded to give us chapter and verse on what the special effects were. It was still a good show though.

GLENN WILLIAMS

Two weeks earlier (10 May), I had seen Sabbath at the Hammersmith in London as the support band was Girlschool, and I was going to every gig of theirs I could at the time. I was hanging around the backstage door waiting for

Black Sabbath

the girls to arrive with a few other fans when we were taken aback by a very familiar figure strolling down the alley next to the theatre towards us – Tony Iommi. Dressed from head-to-toe in black, with a massive silver cross hanging around his neck, he was exactly as you would expect. He said a quick hello and showed us all his guitar before disappearing through the backstage door. That was a good moment, and the gig was good, but Ronnie James Dio was obviously nervous, having only just joined the band. It didn't matter as I was there to see Girlschool anyway.

Fast forward two weeks and this time the support band were Shakin' Street, a French band who I must admit, didn't impress me very much. After two songs, I headed to the bar for a couple of pints of beer. An hour or so later, the intro tape of 'Supertzar' built up to a crescendo over the PA and I started to edge my way to the front.

I was there by the time 'War Pigs' started, and this time, as opposed to the Hammersmith show, Ronnie was much more confident; the band was an aural assault, playing with more freedom knowing that their new singer was settled in. From where I stood, I could smell the smoke from Geezer's cigarette, I could see Bill's beers behind him. I touched Ronnie's shoe when he put his foot on the monitor, and for a few seconds, Tony looked at me… did he recognise me from outside the Hammersmith Odeon? The set list was the same as the Hammersmith, although Ronnie did explain at this one that 'N.I.B.' stood for 'Nativity in Black' (something that Geezer has since denied).

There were several despondent comments from some fans when the houselights went up at the end of the show ('He's not Ozzy!'), but I didn't care. Tony Iommi had looked at *me*, and the thrill I got thinking he may have recognised me was going to carry me home that night.

WHITESNAKE & G-FORCE
26 MAY 1980

ALAN ROBERTS

Whitesnake returned, to my joy, and support was announced as G-Force, Gary Moore's new band. Being a total Lizzy freak, I bought a seat in the balcony and took along my *Black Rose* and *Back on the Streets* album covers hoping to sneak backstage through the upstairs entrance. After failing at the left side, I managed to sweet talk the elderly lady acting as security on the right into letting me in to get Gary to sign for 'my friend who is really ill and might die'.

I joyfully slipped down the stairs to find Gary's dressing room. I knocked.

Photo - Paul Smith

Gary Moore with G-Force

David Coverdale of Whitesnake

Gary opened the door and before I could hand him the pen he exclaimed quite loudly, 'Who the FUCK are you? FUCK OFF!'

Oops.

Whitesnake were good though.

JAMES HUDSON

My cousin, the late Jon Lord, was a member of Whitesnake, but is more well known as a founding member of Deep Purple. Jon was born and bred in Leicester, as I am. His grandfather was my grandfather's brother.

Jon's dad, Reg Lord, was probably in his seventies at the time, still living in the original family home in Leicester. He knew I was a schoolboy and into heavy metal. He invited me to go with him to see Jon when his band were appearing at De Mont. I was thrilled. I went with Reg and had a backstage pass. Going through the crowd at the stage door, I felt so important!

I was in awe when I met the whole band backstage before the concert, with drinks and food. All I remember is this group of big long-haired men like David Coverdale and Ian Paice filling the room with other band members and Jon. I was a shy 15-year-old and didn't say much, but the memory of it is so clear.

I watched the concert, sitting with Jon's dad in the audience. I remember noticing his dad had cotton wool in both his ears. When I asked him why he said it was too 'too bloody loud' for him otherwise!

GOIN' DOWN DE MONT: A PEOPLE'S HISTORY

THIN LIZZY
11 JUNE 1980

TIM CHAMBERS, AGE 15

I discovered Thin Lizzy thanks to my friend's brother. We used to sneak into his room and listen to his Queen collection but one day there was a new album, *Jailbreak*. Wow – this was a lot heavier than Queen, and in my opinion better. I was sold. That Christmas, I got *Live and Dangerous* and after that there was no looking back. After bugging my grandad to go and see them live (me being a young 15-year-old) off I popped to Way Ahead Records in Nottingham to buy tickets. I wasn't allowed the coach travel package as a condition of me going was that I was dropped off and picked up.

There were four of us – myself, Paul, Stef and his brother Andrew. The show was amazing and it was great seeing all these rockers in denim and leather who were so much older than us in our brand new Levi's jackets. So my cut off battle jacket was born. Most of the evening was a blur but I was caught up in the atmosphere, which was electric. It's amazing how quickly you could pick up the words to some of the songs.

After the gig, we were stood somewhere at the back and waiting to be picked up when who should appear from a rear exit but Phil. Talk about being starstruck! He spent about ten minutes talking to us about the gig and thanked us for coming and then he was ushered away. If I wasn't sold on them before I was then. My love affair with Lizzy had begun. I've seen Thin Lizzy a few times since, but sadly without Phil and to be honest it wasn't the same. In my opinion Lizzy are the most underrated rock band ever.

IRON MAIDEN
17 JUNE 1980

SHAUN KNAPP

This was the first of three incredible gigs within five days. They came in at a grand total of £9.50 – £42 in today's money, which was a lot of cash in those days, especially as I'd just left school and was skint.

I really wanted to see them all though, so I sold a few albums and borrowed some cash. Along with some friends, I bought a ticket for Van Halen, slipped the doorman a quid for Iron Maiden (this was a regular thing – they'd usually let you in after the support act) and sneaked into Rush, disappearing into the standing section whilst being chased by the doormen. I picked up a seating ticket stub off the floor as a souvenir. I still have the tickets and the Van Halen tour shirt.

We'd watched Iron Maiden support Judas Priest a few months prior on their *British Steel* tour, and they were great, so this was another chance to see them. The gig formed part of their first headline tour. I don't remember there being a lot of people there, which was disappointing, but I do remember the hall was very hot. A good gig though, with a great light show and Paul Di'Anno on vocals.

BRUCE PEGG

The so-called New Wave of British Heavy Metal was getting ready to explode, and nowhere was it more evident than at this show. Maiden had sold out, and rumour had it that Paul Di'Anno, Maiden's singer, was pulling fans in through the dressing room window. The band's attempts at showmanship were evident even at this early stage of their career, with a roadie emptying a fire extinguisher through a crude cardboard cutout of the band's mascot's (Eddie's) head, which was stationed above the drum kit.

VAN HALEN
20 JUNE 1980

ALAN ROBERTS

The weekend of 20 and 21 June 1980 was one of the most memorable of my life. Not only were Van Halen scheduled for the Friday, but the amazing Rush were playing the day after.

On the first night, entry was secured by the traditional use of a bent coat hanger and a lot of luck. Van Halen were pushing their new album *Women and Children First*, but it had proved rather a disappointment on first listen.

I pushed through to the front, facing Dave Lee Roth as the band went into 'Take Your Whisky Home', and I noticed a bottle of Jack Daniels next to the monitor wedge. As soon as Roth turned to one side I grabbed the bottle and chugged down several gulps… of cold tea. I had discovered his stage-prop!

Unfortunately, Roth sang like he had imbibed at least a bottle of the real stuff and the gig was only saved by the genius of Eddie Van Halen. One moment that made me laugh was when Roth announced bass player Michael Anthony's birthday and a cake was brought out while 'Happy Birthday' was sung… just like every other date on the tour!

SHAUN KNAPP

This was part of their *World Invasion* Tour (also dubbed the *Party 'Till You Die* tour) and we really couldn't believe that they were playing in Leicester. We were all so excited! Eddie Van Halen's 'Eruption' was jaw-dropping. Dave Lee Roth covered every inch of the stage, and I might be wrong, but I'm sure the curtain at the back of Alex Van Halen caught fire during his drum solo. They also used a state-of-the-art sound system and light show, which was really good. The other thing I remember about the gig was that it got absolutely slated by the *Leicester Mercury* the following day. We couldn't believe it – who was this idiot?

DEBORAH ROBERTS

I grew up in Leicester in a family of a musicians. We had been encouraged to explore all genres, and the preferred venue for seeing the different up-and-coming bands introducing themselves to the world was the De Montfort Hall, a beautiful building set in the grounds of Victoria Park. It is here my story unfolds.

On a whim, after a week of spending time with my friends in the evenings and preparing ourselves for the weekly Uni hard rock dance that we lived for, we decided to buy tickets for Van Halen's *Women and Children First* tour. We were unsuccessful. They were sold out.

Nevertheless, we decided to go anyway. We spent the evening before the concert plaiting each other's hair in tiny little plaits to give us that Stevie Nicks/Christine McVie, *Crystal Tipps and Alistair* look that we all craved. The best of times, listening to King Crimson and chatting about how fun it would be to get the boys from the band to let us in. Then, as we did every Friday for the Uni hard rock night, we exchanged clothes to make sure we had the hippest and cool looks that we could muster. I nicked my mum's pure white Afghan coat from her wardrobe for the occasion.

We were young, fair and not unattractive, so entrance was rarely an issue. After some Dutch courage on the bus (a couple of cans of Strongbow and a Saracen's Head lager), we arrived primed and ready to work our female magic.

There were never many people at the back of the De Mont before the shows, just a few girls like us, posing as groupies but with none of the intentions. My friend threw a rock at the backstage windows to draw attention to us, but to no avail. Just as we had started to give up, there appeared a man at the backstage door, dressed in an elaborate suede jacket with fringes and beads, wearing very serious prescription lenses. He said, 'Hello girls. Do you want to come in?'

Hurrah! We made it in to see Van Halen. We didn't know who this man was at the time, so we poured through the backstage door, a trio of giggling teenagers, and continued on to the main floor of the De Mont. The venue was absolutely packed. Van Halen had been there two years before with their first album tour, and everyone was in a state of heightened anticipation. We loved the music, loved the band, and we could not wait for them to begin.

First up were a Dutch band named Lucifer's Friend. As the house lights lowered they were introduced. Behind the drum kit? The mystery man from an hour earlier appeared spinning a pair of drumsticks: Herbert Bornholdt, drummer of Lucifer's Friend, the support band for Van Halen that evening! Truthfully, I didn't care too much for Lucifer's Friend at the time, but I have listened to their music since, and I have a new appreciation for them.

Van Halen came on 45 minutes later and absolutely slayed us with 'Jamie's Crying', the best of *Diver Down* and all the new songs from *Women and Children First*, which frankly none of us really cared for.

Months later, I was watching BBC2 with my brother Alan Roberts. It was a Sunday night and there was nothing on the television except the James Last Orchestra show. And who did we spot in the background playing the drums? Herbert Bornholdt! There were belly laughs for days, but I always respected the man's level of musicianship

RUSH
21 JUNE 1980

PAUL CANNY

When it was announced that Rush would be playing the De Mont on 21 June 1980, I knew it would be essential to queue overnight to get tickets and ensure good seats. There was, however, a slight spanner in the works in that, on the night when queueing

Rush at De Mont

would need to commence, I was also going to the De Mont to see Def Leppard and Magnum (27 April 1980). Obviously, I couldn't do both, so I needed to come up with a creative plan to both see the gig and keep my place in the queue. The solution involved getting my dad to stand in the queue for several hours while I went to the De Mont and then take over from him at about 11.30pm that night. Not many dads would've done that, but as a reward I bought him a ticket and at least he managed to see the holy triumvirate and appreciate them in all their live glory.

It's debatable whether my dad was actually a fan of Rush, but he did tend to enjoy most of the music I listened to. He was, however, also a big jazz fan (as was Neil Peart) and loved a good beat, so he certainly enjoyed the Professor's performance on the night, particularly his solo, and was suitably impressed by the musicianship of the band.

I remember one amusing incident from that night. Rachel, my wife, and I had seen Rush three times the previous year and we both commented on how Geddy seemed fitter and more muscular this year. Not being privy to this conversation, my dad later said, 'Isn't the bassist thin!'

SHAUN KNAPP

Rush put in a fantastic performance in yet another sold-out show. I wasn't a huge fan of them to be honest, but I remember this gig purely by the tightness of the set, how uncomfortably hot the De Mont was again, their incredible musicianship, and yet another bloody drum solo.

ALAN ROBERTS

For Rush, I wasn't going to miss a moment so had purchased a ticket and arrived early to get up front and it turned out to be one of the greatest performances I have ever seen anywhere. The truly mammoth set started with the awesome intro to *2112*, played in its entirety. They covered all their albums to date up to *Permanent Waves*. The highlights of the night though were, for me, the splendour of 'Jacob's Ladder' and the amazing choice of encore, 'La Villa Strangiato'.

Afterwards Geddy and Neil sat behind a table by the merchandise stall and silently signed my programme. We were instructed not to ask questions but just say hello. After the gig I had just witnessed, I couldn't believe how impersonal and, frankly, rude the situation was after regularly being welcome into dressing rooms at previous gigs. I held a grudge for years.

STEVE HACKETT
23 JUNE 1980

STEVE HACKETT

I remember playing there when I'd just had a nasty article written about me when punk was at its height and progressive music was getting a lot of flak. I went on stage expecting the pillory, but actually the audience cheered right the way through the performance, and I felt re-validated. It was great to play there on the *Seconds Out & More* tour, too [10 September 2021]. The crowd reaction was brilliant once again!

Steve Hacket in action in 1980

Photo - Paul Smith

GOIN' DOWN DE MONT: A PEOPLE'S HISTORY

AC/DC
20 & 21 OCTOBER 1980

JO TOWLSON

When I was quite young, my dad, bless him, took us to most gigs and waited for us so we were safe. He used to chat to security while he waited. One time, they kindly offered to let him come in and have a cuppa. When we found him after the show, he told us he'd been sitting with a right twat in the bar – a grown man dressed like a school kid and in shorts too. But then he left to go on stage. Dad thought he must have been in a pantomime or something. 'Oh my God, Dad', I said. 'Did you get his autograph for me? That was Angus. He's in the band!'

'Why would I do that?' Dad said. 'The bloke was an idiot. In fact, if that's the kind of thing they portray I don't want you going again.'

Needless to say, we went again, several times. Minus Dad.

Angus Young of AC/DC

Photos - Paul Smith

GOIN' DOWN DE MONT: A PEOPLE'S HISTORY

THE JAM
12 & 13 NOVEMBER 1980

GAVIN JONES

I'd been to Bingley Hall in Birmingham on the 11th without a ticket, got into the sound check but got rushed out before I could ask to get on the guest list, so bought a ticket off a tout outside at the last minute. They were at the De Mont on the 12th, so when I woke up that morning, ears still buzzing from the night before, I knew I had to go, ticket or not. I set off about lunchtime (I lived about an hour from Leicester) and parked up in a side street in my orange Beetle, then went to the Hall.

This is a big hall set in grounds with a wall around and locked gates, but I managed to squeeze through and went to the side of the building where the three Renault Artics were and where the roadies were milling about. I walked through a side door to a sort of cafe on the side of the hall, and sat in there trying to look like I should be there.

About ten other kids turned up and we were all chatting and sharing Jam stories when I saw Ray and Mick outside, Scousers I had met at the Manchester Apollo a couple of weeks before. I invited them into the cafe and learned they had bunked the train from Liverpool on a platform ticket, as ever drawn to The Jam like a moth to flame! We had a couple of hours to kill until the 3.30pm sound check, so went for some chips, and then went back waiting for the sound check with about 40 other kids.

Big Ken came to the door and let us in, where we walked past Paul, resplendent in his long black corduroy coat and paisley scarf, playing an old piano that was in the hallway with Rick and Bruce, who stood drinking lager. During a lull in the soundcheck while Rick messed with his drums, Paul came to the front of the stage and we asked him if we could get on the guest list. As we'd been to a few sound checks he recognised us and said he'd put us on the list but couldn't give us a pass as he'd none left. This was great, but also gave you trepidation that he would remember to put you on when you didn't have anything solid.

After a couple of hours in a pub, we went back and there was a queue around the block, but we walked straight to the front and said we were on the list (fingers crossed), and there were our names and we went straight in. Thanks, Paul!

After watching the Dolly Mixtures and Piranhas, eventually The Jam came on, introduced by John, and it was a barnstorming set. They were really up for it – they played most of *Sound Affects* mixed in with older songs, kicking off with 'Monday', with Paul's Steve Marriott hair style blowing up as the stage fan kept him cool. They encored with 'Tube Station', 'David Watts', 'When You're Young' and 'Billy Hunt' – all brilliant.

After dodging the security, we waited by the backstage door, and the group came out to chat with us and about 20 other kids. After chatting with Paul about *Sound Affects* and of course politics, we went over to see Rick, who was on his own, and asked him for a guest pass for the next night. He said he'd give us some at the sound check the next day, so I said Ray and Mick could stay at my place, and we went the next day as well.

True to his word, at the sound check the next day we called Rick over and he gave us three guest passes. Someone asked Paul afterwards if they had done any older stuff on the tour, and he said they had done 'In the City' a couple of times, so I said cheekily to him that it would be great if they played that tonight as it was always a great one to see them play with loads of energy.

We had more food, and then it was back to the gig to see supports Kids Next Door and Piranhas again. They weren't my favourites, so we went into the foyer to watch kids come in. I saw some mates from home, Chillo and Steve. They had paid a kid a fiver for his name on the guest list and couldn't believe it worked, as they rushed into the crowd.

Soon enough The Jam came on with a slightly different set, encoring with 'Tube Station', 'David Watts', "A' Bomb', 'When You're Young' and, yes, 'In the City'.

We had a chat with John Weller, Paul's dad and the band's manager, afterwards who showed us the European dates in case we could get to any. I didn't manage to in the end as I lost my job that December.

I dropped Ray and Mick off near the M6 in the freezing rain for them to hitch back to Liverpool. I was sure we would meet up at another Jam gig somewhere. Life was so different then with no mobile phones, phone cameras, etc. to keep in touch, but we seemed to manage.

GOIN' DOWN DE MONT: A PEOPLE'S HISTORY

TIM FILOR

This was the third time I'd seem them. I went with my mate Chris Lazzari. We, plus a lot of the audience, were now living the Mod lifestyle. Chris and I both had scooters and lived in parkas and Mod suits. It had all come clear to me now why, at the Jam show at Loughborough University, we had seen a parka-clad boy taking a beating. I'd had a few close calls myself. The popularity of The Jam was now on an upwards surge and they usually did a two-nighter at Leicester. I hadn't left getting the tickets that late as I worked near the ticket office, but I was disappointed as the only tickets left were in the balcony, sitting down for both nights. I always liked being in the stalls.

The night before the gig, Chris was taken ill and he didn't think he would be

The Jam ticket and autographs

well enough to go, so I offered the ticket to another mate, Pete Barratt. We started off in the balcony but we could see that it was more fun in the stalls. The Jam came on and it was crazy at the front part of the stalls. Pete had also been a punk and liked leaping about, so we decided we wanted a piece of the action. We went downstairs and sneaked into the back of the stalls.

We gradually weaved nearer the front. New songs from the *Sound Affects* album rang out as we slowly edged forward. We were getting pretty close to our objective when the opening riff of 'In the City' started up. It was like a catalyst for us, bearing in mind our previous love of punk, and we started leaping about like madmen. I don't think it went down too well with those around us but we didn't care – this was what we had come for. I can't remember how much more of the gig was left, but we bounced around till the final chords of the encore faded out.

I think we were both pretty knackered at the end, and I started to make my way out with the rest of the crowd. Pete grabbed me and suggested we hang around. We wandered around the hall while it emptied, avoiding the stewards. I was a getting a bit nervy but Pete persuaded me to hang on. The other people in the hall had permits of one sort or another.

What happened next left me gobsmacked. Bruce and Rick came out and stood very close to us and a small crowd gathered round them. We had to get an autograph, but all we had was our ticket stubs, so that's what we handed over. They kindly took them out of our sweaty hands and somehow we managed to get both signatures on them.

We needed the full set, but where was Paul? We had a little wander and found him in another part of the hall, leaning up against a pillar. He looked a bit sullen and a fan was speaking in his ear, something about 'prima donna'.

Pete very politely asked Paul if he'd sign our stubs, and a few seconds later we'd got the full set. It was a magical end to a brilliant night. It just showed how well the lads treated the fans. How many bands at that same level of fame would have come out like that after the gig? Not many, I suspect!

YES
24 & 25 NOVEMBER 1980

CARL LIQUORISH
This was the *Drama* tour when Geoff Downes had taken over on keyboards and Trevor Horn took over the unenviable task of replacing Jon Anderson on vocals. I recall the music starting, and just as Horn

GOIN' DOWN DE MONT: A PEOPLE'S HISTORY

stepped up to the mic for the first time someone shouted, 'Don't be shy!' I understand Horn was very nervous on the tour, but they put on a great show and his contribution was better than most expected it to be. It still sounds good to this day.

Photos – Paul Smith

Chris Squire (top) and Steve Howe & Trevor Horn of Yes, 1980

RICHARD HOUGHTON

I've only ever walked out of two gigs. One was a U2 concert when I was at Uni. They were up-and-coming and the crowd was bouncing around, but I'd had several pints and a bad case of the munchies, so I left the venue to try and find a burger and didn't bother going back. I was sober when I walked out of the Yes gig. I wasn't massively familiar with their catalogue, but I did know that while I might have sat it out to hear Jon Anderson belt out 'Yours is No Disgrace' and 'Roundabout', I wasn't prepared to do it for Trevor after hearing the first couple of songs. My willingness to give him a decent crack of the whip wasn't helped by it being all seated gig and me having a view that was partially obstructed by one of the metal pillars in the Hall.

Photo - Richard Bent

Rory Gallagher (year unknown)

Pye Hastings of Caravan (1977)

Photo - Mark Healey

Mark Healey's badge collection

KK Downing of Judas Priest (1979)

Gillan (1980)

Ray Davies of the Kinks (1981)

Paul Chapman of UFO (1982)

Michael Schenker Group (1981)

Jon Anderson (1980)

MADNESS
21 DECEMBER 1980

TERRY PRICE
This was my first ever gig. It was Christmas 1980 – the Nutty Boys Christmas tour – and I was 11. The support act was a magician! All the skinheads started spitting at him, and it became a bit hostile until Chaz Smash came and asked the crowd to ease up. The magician stormed off, but Madness played a blinder!

TIMOTHY FILOR
We went in a big group from my village and were a bit boisterous as it was near Christmas. We sang Madness songs on the bus all the way into town. We were very near the front of the stage, and I remember people getting up on the stage. Somebody broke the bass player's guitar strap, and he had to sit down for the rest of the gig which he wasn't very happy about. Terry Hall joined them during the encore to sing the song 'Madness'.

SLADE
9 MARCH 1981

STEVE PRESTON
I went to the De Mont with a friend to see Slade during their *Till Deaf Do Us Part* tour in 1981. Deaf was a good description. The sound had my ears ringing for three days afterwards. Noddy came onto a pitch-black stage at the start with one spotlight on him. He was dressed all in black with a vicar's collar on. His words? 'For what you are about to receive, God 'elp ya!' Then all hell broke loose. Fantastic gig.

STEELEYE SPAN
6 APRIL 1981

TIM RABONE
It was Thatcherite Britain, meaning that, until we could get out, me and my punk mates had no money, no prospects and – it turns out mistakenly

– no future. In our travels up and down New Walk, a young and merry (whatever he was on, it must have been quite potent) Grebo lad had attached himself to our group.

As we neared the De Mont, we noticed the concert had started and that, unusually, there were hardly any security staff on the doors. Having nothing else better to do, and no idea what band was playing, we tried a side door which opened on first shove, and without any checks whatsoever, we walked into the auditorium where Steeleye Span were in mid-jig (or reel or whatever), and where a full audience of mid-thirties yuppie types were seated in orderly rows on folding chairs, clapping along wholeheartedly.

I distinctly remember the impression that most of the yuppie gals had Nolans-type haircuts and long, floral-printed skirts while most of the yuppie blokes for some reason had cardigans draped over their shoulders. Needless to say, our leather-jacketed, spiky-haired entourage and the grinning Grebo stood out a little, and though security, who may have been short-staffed or already pissed, didn't challenge us, we took ourselves off to one side of the Hall just to watch the audience more than anything.

I think things would have gone fine and we would have just quietly made our exit after a short while had not been for Maddy Prior and her decision at that point to come down from the stage and skip around the aisles in the hall, encouraging the audience to join her in that faux ceilidh-type dancing that they all seemed to enjoy (only the yuppie gals joined in).

Whatever switch kicked in for our Grebo friend kicked in almost instantly as he decided it would enhance the experience for everyone if, with a well-aimed cowboy boot, he were to trip Ms Prior in mid-skip and presumably send her sprawling. Luckily, he was so merry that the first time he let fly, Maddy was a full yard and a half past him, so she didn't even notice. It was when we saw her coming around for a second circuit, with Grebo becoming decidedly more determined that he'd get her this time, that we took action and bundled him out of the hall and out through the door via which we'd come in, despite his protestations that he liked her and that he just wanted to dance with her.

We laughed and shook hands. Grebo staggered off across Vicky Park, and we headed back down New Walk to see if anyone was in the Bricklayers' Arms.

GOIN' DOWN DE MONT: A PEOPLE'S HISTORY

ORCHESTRAL MANOEUVRES IN THE DARK
15 APRIL 1981

ANDREW LIDDLE, OMD LIGHTING DESIGNER

Instead of staying in the Leicester city centre, the band decided to stay in a little village outside, at the Quorn Country Hotel, where my girlfriend was a chambermaid. Entering one of the keyboard player's rooms in the morning, she was enticed to get into bed. Bearing in mind they've got two keyboard players, I couldn't possibly comment which one.

They turned up later in my local for a pint, where I first met McCluskey and got told to 'fuck off, Andrew.' Years later, being interviewed for my job, he asked, 'Is there anything else?' I said, 'Yeah, you're allowed one 'Fuck off, Andrew' a day.' I'm Andrew and he's Andy. He explained this to me on our first meeting, saying, 'There's only room for one Andy around here.' So I said, 'Right, fuck it. I'll be Andrew from now on.'

GIRLSCHOOL
28 APRIL 1981

GLENN WILLIAMS

I was one of the original BGA – the Barmy Girlschool Army – and by this point, I was close to amassing seeing a hundred of their gigs up and down the UK. Thursday night, sometime earlier in the year, *Sounds* had dropped through my letterbox and their new tour dates were advertised. I was ecstatic to see they were playing De Mont, their first time headlining in Leicester, and on Enid's birthday!

It was a Tuesday and I had taken a few days off work. It was one of those magical English spring days; the sky was blue and cloudless and the sun was glorious. Some of my Barmy Army mates were coming to Leicester for the gig – Kenny Tubby had been with me the night before in Birmingham and kipped on my mum and dad's sofa. By lunchtime, we were in the Marquis Wellington. Around 2pm we went to the De Mont. The girls had already arrived and were doing a photoshoot for *Flexipop* magazine in the grounds and dressing rooms. We said hello to the crew, made sure Tim (Warhurst, their tour manager) had put us on the guest list, and went into town.

I can't remember who had the idea, but one of us suggested we should get Enid flowers and we somehow found a florist who said they would deliver two dozen red roses around 7pm. We were back in the Marquis at opening time.

At the gig, I was buzzing all night. Loads of my mates were in the audience, the BGA was out in force, and the girls were onstage. Two songs from the end, Ken and I went backstage and waited in the wings. They finished the set and I walked on and presented Enid with her bouquet. The crowd sang 'Happy Birthday', and I was grinning from ear to ear.

Ken and I went back out in the audience with the BGA for the encore, had a quick chat with the girls backstage afterwards ('See you in Bristol on Friday!') and then caught last orders at the Marquis before we all headed to our various homes. I've never been so happy in my life.

THE TUBES
25 JUNE 1981

MARK HEALEY

By now, Glenn Williams was getting more and more involved with the backstage side of things and had gradually been taking steps into becoming a roadie. Because of this, he had become quite well connected with promoters and crews. This time, I convinced Glenn that we should go, but Glenn said that he could get me on the guest list!

I had heard of them. I knew they had interesting and outrageous stage shows, but I knew nothing about their music except for one track. But being on the guest list and getting in for free wasn't something I was going to turn down. Glenn said, 'Just turn up, give them your name, and I'll meet you inside.'

I turned up at the entrance doors of the Hall and said to one of the staff that I was on the guest list. I even took on the part by semi-pretending that I was important! I half expected to be turned down flat, but he took a piece of paper out of his pocket and there indeed was my name. I just strolled through nonchalantly like I had done the same thing a thousand times.

The concert was standing downstairs, and Glenn saw me near the stage and joined me to watch the concert. The show started and the band had only played a few notes when suddenly their lead singer came to the edge of the stage and pointed to a girl in the audience that he seemingly recognised and shouted at her. The music stopped and he dramatically leapt off the stage and into the crowded audience. The audience scattered around him to give him space. We were all gobsmacked, even shocked – never had anything like this happened before. He grabbed the girl very physically and appeared to assault her and then chased her, forcing her onto to the stage itself.

It was at this point that we and the rest of the audience began to realise that it was all just part of the act. We had been deliberately set up. They had lived up to their reputation for being outrageous!

ORCHESTRAL MANOEUVRES IN THE DARK
15 NOVEMBER 1981

JAN GOULD

I first noticed them on *Top of the Pops* with 'Enola Gay'. I finished my O levels that summer, but unemployment was high and I couldn't get a job. I reluctantly started A levels. I was officially studying Maths, Economics and Sociology but it wasn't long before OMD became my fourth subject (fan club card 3255). My best friend Mirelle and I studied together. Boring maths lectures on a Wednesday morning were vastly improved by inserting a fresh copy of *Smash Hits* into my A4 folder. Collecting pictures, posters and lyrics became a weekly ritual. Every folder and textbook was covered with them.

To say I wasn't a natural academic is an understatement. Part of my survival plan was to find ways of integrating my favourite subject, OMD, into my school week. Mirelle and I were shipped to school from nearby villages, but luckily my auntie and uncle lived close to our school and considerately gave us the key to their house, use of their hi-fi and storage of our vinyl. The new charts were announced on a Tuesday lunchtime, when I luckily had a free period followed by lunch. I'd escape to my auntie's whilst Mirelle would rush round as the charts were being announced after her chemistry lesson.

Later that year we decided to see both OMD and Depeche Mode live. Depeche was supposed to be my first, but Mum and Dad wouldn't let me go, thinking the students might cause trouble. We had a few heated discussions about that. OMD at Leicester's De Montfort Hall was my first 'proper' concert. I'll always remember the excitement and energy of that gig. Towards the end we moved to the back of the venue and witnessed the audience going wild as the final 'chug-chugs' of 'Stanlow' signalled the end of a great night.

Coincidentally, my most recent OMD gig was also with Mirelle at Leicester De Montfort Hall on 5 November 2017. Thirty-six years later, we're still best friends and I'm again watching the crowd go wild as another great evening comes to an end.

THIN LIZZY
14 DECEMBER 1981

CHRIS BIRT
A friend rang to say he had two tickets to see Thin Lizzy that Friday night. Being a rock music fan, I'd always liked the hits and I thought that Phil looked cool. Well, that Friday night changed my outlook on music. It was the *Renegade* tour with Snowy White, Scott Gorham, Brian Downey and this front man who just had the crowd in his hand. I can honestly say that they were the best live rock band I've ever seen. They just blew me away – two blazing guitars, a drummer who was fantastic and this Irish bass player who had every woman in there purring.

PAUL SMITH
I arranged to meet my friend travelling on the train from Sheffield, due in to Leicester in plenty of time. The train got stuck somehow just outside of Leicester and arrived two to three hours late. There were no mobile phones, of course, so there was no way of communicating. We missed the show, but we did make the pub for last orders.

GOIN' DOWN DE MONT: A PEOPLE'S HISTORY

THE JAM
22 & 23 MARCH 1982

GAVIN JONES

After a great gig at Birmingham a couple of nights before, it was off to the De Mont for another two! I took Lisa to this one, and you could tell things had got bigger for The Jam now, as we had to wait ages for Kenny to let us in the sound check, and we all got kicked out before they had finished – no chance of the guest list here, but luckily I had got tickets for these two gigs!

My tickets were for the seats upstairs, a first for me, and Lisa went to sit with a friend so I was all on my own and a bit bored watching the support. They didn't seem to have the charged atmosphere like normal, or was I just getting old? There was a girl poet on first, and then the support Rudi, who were okay, and then – at last – The Jam came on.

Once again, similar to Brum a couple of nights earlier, they did a frantic, electrifying set. At one point, Paul smashed his Telecaster into his Vox amplifier. They did three encores after doing most of *The Gift* and some of *Setting Sons* and *Sound Affects*.

I hung around afterwards and got my *Sound Affects* songbook signed by them all. I had a chat with John Weller about going to Brussels in April, which I signed up for on a coach trip.

Home by midnight, some sleep then ready to go back again for the next one!

The following night, I went on my own. I got to the sound check early afternoon and they ran through a few songs. They kept screwing up 'Dreams of Children', before getting it right on the third attempt. Then they didn't play it in the gig! Paul had a horrible pink Telecaster which I hadn't seen before, but he didn't use that in the gig and I never saw it again!

After getting some chips, I met my mates Hoppy and Mac in a pub nearby. They were getting ready to see The Jam for the first time, and I was hoping it would be a good gig for them after they had put up with me going on about them for the past few years saying how good they were live!

Unfortunately, it turned out to be probably the worst Jam gig I ever went to. At one point the sound equipment packed up and they had to stop for a few minutes while it was sorted out. The set, including one encore, only lasted just under an hour, and you could tell they weren't happy on stage. A lot of the crowd were a bit pissed off as well.

I didn't bother trying to get in at the end, as I thought they wouldn't be in the mood for much of a chat. I caught up with Hoppy and Mac and assured them that this was a bad one and they were normally much better. Having said that, they still thought they were great, so even a bad Jam gig was miles better than most other things.

TIM FILOR

It was now March 1982. I wasn't quite so young, but I was free and single. A live Jam fix was needed again asap. I didn't have to wait long for them to visit the De Mont. My old mate Steve kept me company for the second time. I could only get balcony seats again, which was a bit of a bummer, but we were near the stage so it wasn't too bad. There was no chance of getting in the stalls this time, as security had been tightened and you had to show your ticket to get in. As we looked down we could see the Mods sweltering in their parkas. They seemed so young, probably only 14 or 15.

The Jam came on and the room yet again erupted. They were huge now. We didn't know at the time that it was close to ending – we just sat back and enjoyed the ride. A constant stream of little Mods were getting pulled out of the front as the crowd surged forward. They had a brief moment with their heroes on stage before being hauled off by the bouncers.

The band had lots of material to choose from now and a new album to promote. I'd like to say I can remember what they did but my memory is coloured by a video I have of virtually the same set at New Bingley Hall. The backdrop was a banner saying 'Transglobal Unity Express'. I can remember them doing that song and also 'Scrape Away', which seemed to be extra-long, 'Pretty Green', 'Man at the Corner Shop' and finally 'Happy Together'.

We left the gig elated and made a quick dash to the Old Horse on London Road to catch last orders. It was a real spit-and-sawdust pub in those days but was later refurbished. I must have been full of adrenalin as I never rush anywhere normally.

As we supped our beers, we never really thought that would be the last time we would see the band live but, sadly, it was. I didn't get to see any of the final gigs and had to be content with the final outing on *The Tube*. I have to admit that once the boys had unofficially expanded to five it wasn't quite the same for me, but with hindsight, you can now see where Paul wanted to go.

All I can say is, massive thanks to The Jam. It was good while it lasted. The legacy for me is that it inspired me to get back in a band with three other Jam fans. I obviously never found fame and fortune, but I did carry on playing in various line ups till 1997. Over that period of time I met my wife, made a lot of my friends, and have two great kids and a lot of memories.

MOTÖRHEAD
7 & 8 APRIL 1982

ANDY SAVAGE

Motörhead and Hawkwind were yearly events for the rockers amongst us. Before the *Iron Fist* show, I had some shots from the doctor for foreign travel – the top of my arm was very painful and swollen, and being in the crowd was annoying and hurt. But I spent the entire gig boogying with the music, and then I stuck my head into one of the speaker bins. I couldn't hear anything clearly for three days afterwards. Such are our memories.

SIMPLE MINDS
12 DECEMBER 1982

CAROL LOUDON

My favourite band was, and still is, Simple Minds who I first heard when I used to go to Echies nightclub on Church Gate. I bought their albums and then it was announced they were touring. The day the tickets went on sale, I went down early to the box office in Town Hall Square to queue as that was the only way to buy tickets then. It feels so long ago! There was only myself and one other person, so I got ticket numbers 1, 2, 3 and 4.

On the day of the gig it was snowing, but I still dragged my sister, brother and niece down to the De Mont for half past four so I could be at the front. The gig itself was everything I hoped, and I was lucky enough to get the set list off the stage (which someone on Simple Minds fan group on Facebook said was definitely written by Jim Kerr). I didn't do the stage door thing as I had my young niece with me, but my friend did and told them about me, and Jim Kerr wrote me the note. All my Christmases came at once!

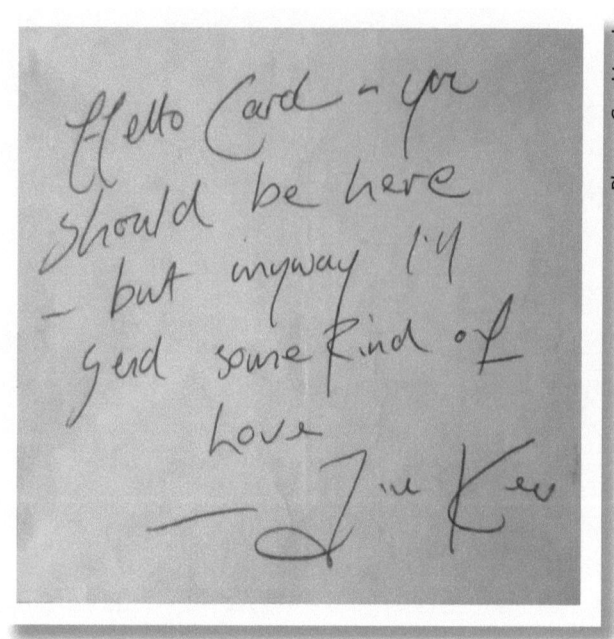

Jim Kerr's message to Simple Minds fan Carol

THIN LIZZY
17 FEBRUARY 1983

CHRIS NOON

Back then a coach trip would come through towns and village to pick up concert goers so me, Mike Baldwin, Phil Britten and Bob Bonafin waited on a cold late February afternoon for the coach. The coach arrived and the excitement increased, giggling and arsing about all the way to Leicester.

We got into the venue and I headed straight to the merch stand. One t-shirt, scarf, studded wristband and programme later, I made my way to my seat. In no time the support act was announced and Mama's Boys took to the stage, Pat McManus absolutely dominating proceedings and the band was knocking some great music out for over 30 minutes. They left the stage and it was almost time.

My heart was pounding. Finally the lights went down, my giddyometer went up to twelve and in a flash the boys were there, right in front of me – Thin FUCKING Lizzy!

Opening with 'Thunder and Lightning', I was in heaven and jumping up and down like a lunatic. The songs came and went. I can't remember what songs were next but I do remember stopping and taking in the moment. It was magical. The light bouncing off Phil's mirror scratch plate, John Sykes absolutely shredding his Les Paul and flashing his blond mane, the sublime Scott Gorham making it all look too easy, Downey holding them all together and Wharton giving Lizzy the keyboard fill that was so important to the last two albums. It wasn't too loud, it wasn't quiet, it was perfect.

The songs kept coming, classic after classic until the final song, 'Rosalie'. Then it was finished – over. That was it. I'd witnessed one of the greatest bands to ever walk the planet and then came the post-gig blues. We all sat on the coach on the way back in silence. No more Lizzy. But the story wasn't over for me because 38 years later, going through some boxes brought out from the loft, I came across my concert programme (still with the poster intact) and I grinned like a Cheshire cat. It all came back. Like a warm glow, I remembered Thin Lizzy live. The memory never leaves us. Are you out there?

MARK SMIGGY SMITH

I knew it was 'farewell' for Lizzy and the new album didn't come out for another month, so there would be songs that we hadn't heard before, and a new guitarist in John Sykes, of which I had heard nothing before. That February night there were three of us. Angela, myself, and my twelve-year-old nephew, James. Seeing Lizzy for a sixth time, the excitement was off the scale for me, so I can't imagine what it was like for James seeing his first gig.

It was the first time I sat at a concert. A twelve-year-old in the mosh pit may not have ended well. We were in the balcony, close to the stage. The gig started with 'Thunder and Lightning' which was an unknown quantity to me, and very different to what I'd become accustomed to. The gig was a blinder, and I loved every second.

GOIN' DOWN DE MONT: A PEOPLE'S HISTORY

IRON MAIDEN
6 MAY 1983

JO TOWLSON

Once again, I was at the front of the stage. A giant version of Eddie, the band mascot, came on stage and as it was walking across the stage the head fell off!

The blond guitarist, Dave Murray, was in front of me headbanging, and I was covered in baby powder from his hair. It tickled me – these hard men of rock smelling of Johnson's baby talc! The things you remember – I was never a massive fan of them, but you have to see them all, don't you, just to say you've been.

WHAM!
21 OCTOBER 1983

YVONNE GRANT

I was at the front – this was back in the days when you were actually crushed against the stage. My friend fainted, but George Michael held my hand!

KISS
24 OCTOBER 1983

JAMES KERSHAW

This was my first ever Kiss concert. I have maybe seen them 30 or more times since then.

It was a Monday. I was 14 and together with my friend Andy, we bunked off school in Loughborough at lunchtime, took the train to Leicester, then walked up to the hallowed De Montfort Hall for early afternoon. It was our first time hanging around the stage door area pre-show, so we didn't really know what we were doing. Late afternoon, Kiss finally arrived, there were a lot of people, and a lot of noise. I never even saw Eric Carr or Vinnie Vincent at all.

Gene Simmons came strolling past looking just like the enormous

Rock God of Thunder that he was. I got him to sign a copy of the front of that week's *Sounds* that had Kiss on the cover.

Then came Paul Stanley. He exuded confidence and composure and had a real energy about him, but was still great with every fan there. I was starstruck, but still managed to get Paul to sign my *Sounds* cover also.

I had a tiny little camera with me, and just as Paul was about to disappear through the stage door, I shouted 'Hey Paul! Could I get a picture please?' He turned round, thumbs up and in a loud American accent answered 'sure!'

Paul Stanley of Kiss christened James Kershaw his 'English buddy'

Over the next almost 40 years, I probably met the band around ten times (my daughter Em even ended up on stage with Paul at Birmingham's National Indoor Arena in 2017).

I told Paul the Leicester story in 2003 when I met Kiss in Atlanta, Georgia in the USA (while they were on tour with Aerosmith). He loved the story, so I became his 'English Buddy', as it says on the picture that had been taken in Leicester 20 years before.

EWEN

I'd arranged to meet with friends at a Kiss gig at De Montfort Hall. I arrived early, got myself a beer and wandered into the hall, which was empty. I hauled myself up onto the stage for a sit down – you could do that kind of thing back then. You'd be politely asked to move sooner or later.

I'd perched in a spot with my back against the sidefill and the main

PA to my right, chilling out in a comfy corner. Friends appeared and refreshed my beer, as I wasn't going anywhere unless asked, to which I'd reply that I'd had a big day and my legs were tired.

Time passed. The hall filled. Stage lights dimmed. A chap appeared and checked all the mics, then noticed me. I smiled, he kinda hesitated, then smiled back and disappeared. The house lights went out. Then, KISS!

So I got to watch the whole gig from on stage.

The only downer of the night? A guitar was trashed and passed to a friend of a friend in the audience, who was clearly delighted, then immediately accosted by a huge thug who took the guitar.

Several fifteen-year-olds found themselves slightly wiser the next day.

U2
3 DECEMBER 1983

MIKE STANLEY

I remember this gig vividly, and I will till the day I die. It was like an explosion of attitude and power. The Edge was awesome, and Bono scared the living daylights out of everyone when he climbed the amp stack and clung on to the old balcony. When he decided to come back on the stage, the amp stack swayed and nearly toppled.

The sound at the De Mont was always fantastic, and the mixing meant you could actually hear what was being sung. Bono professed that they would never use electronic instruments when The Edge sat down and played the opening to 'October' (a promise I bet he wished he kept when the midi sequencer failed three times three years later at Milton Keynes whilst trying to perform 'Bad'!). Adam's head flung around in time to the pulsing bass throughout 'The Ocean', and he kept it going for bloody ages. Eventually, being the last to leave the stage, he simply put his bass on its stand and coolly walked off. I remember thinking then that I'd just witnessed the best rock band the world has ever seen.

Of course, the whole band stayed behind and came out and spoke to everyone who'd waited for them. They laughed and joked with their fans and signed every autograph asked of them.

Boy George of Culture Club (1983)

Joan Armatrading (1983)

Photos - Paul Smith

Eric Clapton (1983)

Elvis Costello (1983)

Alan Hull of Lindisfarne (1983)

Culture Club (1983)

Photos - Paul Smith

Annie Lennox of the Eurythmics (1983)

TINA TURNER
8 FEBRUARY 1984

EWEN

I went to see Tina Turner. It was an all-seated gig – I hate those – but TINA!

She was incredible, her band phenomenal. A few people got up and went to the front of the stage to dance. Security didn't seem bothered, so others soon followed including me. During the encore she was kissing folks' hands, including mine. I didn't wash for a week. At my second kiss I returned the favour, so I got to swap bodily fluids with her!

I went to dozens of gigs at De Montfort Hall over the years, starting with 10CC when I was 14. But Tina and her band were simply the best.

SIMPLE MINDS
12 MARCH 1984

AJAY MISTRY

I remember the crowd being really, really boisterous to the point where Jim, when he used to introduce and preface some of the songs, demanded that the crowd should 'Be quiet!' and 'Shut up!' on a number of occasions.

'Waterfront' even contained lyrics from Norman Greenbaum's 'Spirit in the Sky', particularly relevant for me since it was the UK number one when I was born. Selfishly, I think of it as a dedication of sorts. And whilst I love the slow version of 'New Gold Dream' from *Live in the City of Light* I will never, ever forget the turbo-charged version they played at the De Mont, laced with lyrics from Talking Heads' version of Al Green's 'Take Me to the River' and The Doors' 'Light My Fire'. Indeed, when Jim was singing, 'C'mon baby light my fire' and repeated 'Fire! Fire!', jabbing the air with his hand, I remember it sounding more like a celebration of fire, rather than something to fear.

Whilst the Minds have never let me down when I've seen them live, I'm convinced the band were spurred on to new heights by the crowd that night. There were times when Jim was just absorbed in the songs, prowling around the stage and looking like he was taking numerous run ups and threatening to make that final glorious leap into the crowd. Perhaps, thankfully for himself, he never did.

Forbes, particularly, was in a world of his own, bouncing up and down and not content with staying to the left of Jim. One second he'd be next to Mel, the next having a joke with Charlie by his shoulder. I walked out of the venue that night absolutely buzzing, ten feet tall.

THE SMITHS
18 MARCH 1984

SHAUN KNAPP

All I can remember about it was that the atmosphere was electric. It was a heady mix of excitement and anticipated violence, which always makes you pay attention.

They really were a top band at the time. They were also a band that were favoured by the Baby Squad (a football hooligan firm linked to Leicester City FC), so there were quite a few tasty characters in the crowd, which added to the atmosphere.

They weren't on for very long. I've been told since that they played 13 songs and I seem to remember that they did three encores. I can recall them playing 'What Difference Does It Make?' like it was yesterday. It was absolutely fantastic. It just sounded so good live, you didn't want it to finish. I've been to lots of gigs, but this was one that stays with you, it was so different to anything that I'd seen at the time. Looking back, it was quite breathtaking really, the audience were so up for it.

The main thing was they were a bloody good live band. Every song played was a winner, and I think we all knew we were watching them at their peak.

GAVIN JONES

Once The Jam split at the end of '82, I was a bit lost gig wise, and the music scene was a bit transitional. Then on a trip over to my girlfriend's house in mid '83 I heard John Peel play 'Hand in Glove', and I was hooked. I was totally into them once 'This Charming Man' came out in late '83, and just had to see them.

I got tickets for De Mont for the 18th March gig in '84, and myself and three mates went in my trusty Beetle. It was totally different to when I'd been to De Mont to see The Jam – no big artics and vans, just a minibus and a couple of small box vans for the gear, and a simple stage set inside. The crowd was a mixture of goth/punk and indie kids, interested to see what all the fuss was about. Even though I had gallery tickets, I went downstairs with the mob, and I was pleased I did. It was a lively crowd and seemed pretty full, and the place erupted when they came on.

Morrissey had his shirt undone, beads on and a few gladioli in his back pocket, and there was a smattering of flowers around the place which added to the vibe. They broke into 'Still Ill' and then 'Reel Around the Fountain', and Moz disappeared, only for me to catch a glimpse of him writhing around on his back on the stage floor singing away. Wow, this was different!

Marr was brilliant, the epitome of the cool rock star in his denim jacket and Jetglo Rickenbacker, jangling out the tunes to perfection, and Rourke and Joyce bashed away at the rhythm to keep it moving along. They did all of the first albums and some singles – I seem to remember them leaving 'This Charming Man' to an encore, though I may be wrong. They did four or five encores anyway to end a mind-blowing gig and herald in the next generation of guitar indie pop.

ORCHESTRAL MANOEUVRES IN THE DARK
19 NOVEMBER 1984

LEE MCNULTY

One of my lasting memories is from the 1984 *Junk Culture* tour. The band was going to play 'Locomotion' next and the Fairlight computer crashed. They didn't panic. Paul went to work, trying to get it back up and running. It seemed to take a long time, but I guess it was only a few minutes.

DIO
2 OCTOBER 1984

JOE DUGGAN

Dio on the *Last in Line* tour, with Queensryche opening, was my first gig. I spent the whole evening squashed up at the front. It was a fantastic night until, during the third encore, someone got onstage and tried to hug Dio, causing him to miss the first line of 'The Mob Rules'. He stopped the show and said, 'I hope you enjoyed that because we didn't,' and walked off. End of show.

FRANKIE GOES TO HOLLYWOOD
15 MARCH 1985

SHAUN KNAPP

This was an eagerly anticipated tour with lots of rumours that they couldn't play live. Tickets cost a whopping £7.50 each (£24 in today's money) and sold out within hours. I remember that they weren't on for very long, but it was a top gig on so many levels – the atmosphere was great, the hall was full and FGTH delivered an incredible show. After all of the hype surrounding the tour, I remember coming out of there feeling ever so slightly ripped off but thinking I'd just seen something a bit special.

THE SMITHS
1 APRIL 1985

GAVIN JONES

I ended up going to a few Smiths gigs around the Midlands, including another one at De Mont in April '85. They were very well established now and at the top of their game, another brilliant gig that I have a couple of standout memories from. When they did 'How Soon is Now?', there was a big backlight behind Moz as he started singing, which gave it loads of atmosphere. And as this was the *Meat is Murder*

Photos - Paul Smith

Steve Howe of Yes (2014)

Chris Squire of Yes (2014)

Fish of Marillion (1984)

'Atomik' Tommy McClendon of UFO (1985)

Photos - Paul Smith

Rick Wakeman (1985)

Ian Anderson of Jethro Tull (2021)

Phil Mogg of UFO (1985)

Freddie & the Dreamers (1985)

tour, when they did the title track the noise of the machinery and cow mooing the speakers at the start sent shivers down your spine, especially when Morrisey came in with the vocal, 'A heifer whines'. An absolutely fantastic night again.

HAWKWIND
28 NOVEMBER 1985

TONY BYKER, GAYE BYKERS ON ACID
We never played at the De Montfort Hall. We did Leicester University and the Charlotte and somewhere else, I think, but the only time I can remember going to the De Mont was when the Gaye Bykers on Acid were just starting and I think it was myself and Kev, the drummer.

We were squatting in Leicester at the time, kind of up near that end of the city, and we went with a bunch of friends to see Hawkwind on their *Chronicles of the Black Sword* tour and of course we all took a bunch of mushrooms. I took the most and I remember getting to the De Montfort Hall and of course it's full of big, burly bikers and Hell's Angels and everybody looked really ominous.

I was really having a bad trip, hallucinating and starting to feel sick, and I started to freak out, so I ended up just wandering around in circles in the park outside. I missed the entire gig just being outside trying to get my head together.

RED WEDGE
(BILLY BRAGG & PAUL WELLER)
28 JANUARY 1986

RICHARD HOUGHTON
I had bought *Life's a Riot with Spy vs Spy* on a whim in Andy's Records in Bedford and was keen to see Billy Bragg live as soon as I could. He was headlining the Red Wedge package tour, which was an anti-Thatcher left wing collective of like-minded musicians who were trying to get young people interested in politics again, with some sort of

backing from the Labour Party. This involved lots of photo ops for then Labour leader Neil Kinnock with different musicians.

I don't know what real impact this grouping had on young people's attitudes to politics, but it did bring together some tasty acts that you wouldn't normally see outside of a festival line up, perhaps only playing a handful of numbers. There was the added attraction of unannounced surprise guests appearing on the tour. At the Newcastle gig, The Smiths famously played. At De Mont we got Paul Weller on backing guitar for a couple of numbers. And I saw Suggs and Chas Smash from Madness at the bar, although I don't recall them making it as far as the stage.

MARILLION
29 JANUARY 1986

NIGEL OAKLEY

I worked in a car spares shop in Beaumont Leys, and Radio Leicester had a phone-in competition to win two tickets and backstage passes to meet the band that night at the De Montfort Hall. Being a

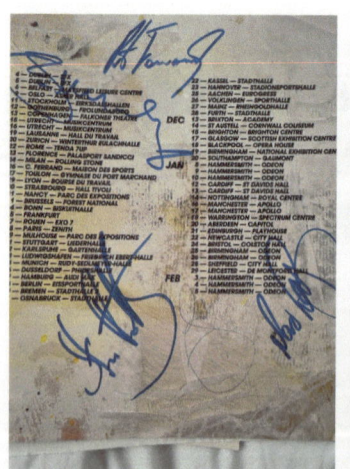
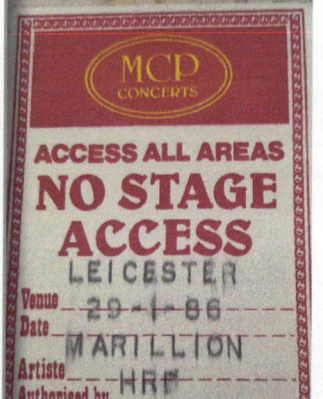

Autographs and a triple A pass for Marillion

massive Marillion fan, I dialed the number as soon as the presenter started asking the question: 'Marillion wrote a love song about a girl called…?' I was the first person to get through and answer, 'Kaleigh!'

OZZY OSBOURNE
3 MARCH 1986

JOE DUGGAN

It was my first time to see Ozzy, so it was an exciting time for 16-year-old me. It was a great gig, but Ozzy peed his pants during the intro to 'Mr Crowley', and then pretended to strangle the unfortunate roadie who came on to clean the stage near the mic stand. Fortunately, he didn't throw the towel into the audience.

BON JOVI
23 NOVEMBER 1986

JO TOWLSON

Jon Bon Jovi was a god. My friend and I were besotted. It was a brilliant tour, they were brilliant live. We went backstage after the show to get autographs, along with every other female in Leicester. But while they were all crowding the door, we spotted the tour bus, so off we went to it.

Our luck was in. Someone had left the back emergency door open, so we climbed aboard. One of the band members was standing in the aisle, and all we could see was his bare bum. We got a fit of giggles and tried hiding in one of the bunks (our mums were going to kill us when they found out, but we didn't care). We were waiting for Jon, shoving our fists in our mouths to stop us giggling, everyone else was on the bus now. We just got a glimpse of 'The God' when this bloody huge security man grabbed us and threw us off the bus!

We lived on that memory for years and still do now: the night we shared Jon Bon Jovi's bunk. So, so many memories of my youth. We went to every single rock and metal concert – we were at the De Mont more than anywhere else, and never really realised how lucky we were.

THE POGUES
14 MARCH 1987

ALAN ROBERTS

This was another storming night watched from the side of the stage. At the soundcheck Shane MacGowan was, let's say, a little worse for wear, and by the time of the gig he was literally legless and had to be carried to the stage from the dressing room.

What I witnessed then is nothing short of a miracle. As soon as his feet hit the stage he transformed and walked graciously to his mic and then proceeded to play a faultless set, all the time swigging away from a whiskey bottle.

As soon as he left the stage, he collapsed again and was carried back to the dressing room.

INXS
8 FEBRUARY 1988

ALAN ROBERTS

Around 1988, I managed to get into the famous Gopher Stage Crew after proving myself with years of experience on the road. Therefore, I was actually allowed to be backstage. I really loved the De Mont, so it was just a joy to go to work. Helping the crew unload, construct and operate the gear before finally stripping it down and load up the trucks after was damn hard work, but we were well paid and had the perk of a free gig to boot.

When INXS came, everyone was excited to hear the band that was taking the world by storm. After a good morning's graft, a few of us sat on a flight case in front of the stage to watch the soundcheck. All was good until Michael Hutchence took to the stage. He glared down at us, then called over the stage manager who promptly headed our way and asked us to leave the auditorium. 'Michael doesn't like people watching him,' he said.

I remember thinking how stupid that sounded as there would be a couple of thousand people doing just that a few hours later!

CAROLE EXON

They were doing a series of small concerts around the UK, and we managed to get tickets for the De Montfort. The Australian cricket team came in to watch them. They were stood behind us, and the lads we were with spoke to them. I don't like cricket, so I had no idea who they were. But it was a great concert.

R.E.M.
17 MAY 1989

STEPHEN WALKER

I'm originally from Sunderland, and it was my second year at Leicester University. My absolute favourite band is R.E.M. and they were playing the De Mont. I'd wanted to see them since their first album in 1980, and they'd toured the UK a few times, but life conspired to make sure I never managed it.

I got a ticket for the De Mont gig. It was the *Green* tour, the album and tour just before they became officially the Biggest Band In The World ('Losing My Religion', etc.). I got a call a week before the gig to tell me my Granda had died. Obviously upset, I had to travel home to Sunderland. The funeral was on the Wednesday, the day after the gig, but I only had public transport, so no way I could do both. I was gutted to miss the gig to be honest, but I had to show my respects, and support my Mam.

It was an awesome gig by all accounts and going by the bootleg tape I picked up later. I never got to see them live, because I don't do stadium gigs or festivals. After the funeral, my Mam said,' You didn't have to come you know, you could have stayed in Leicester. I wouldn't have minded.'

THE STRANGLERS
23 FEBRUARY 1990

ROB TOWNSEND

Three days before this show, I was riding down Rutland Street. I got to the St George's roundabout when I heard a big explosion. It was the IRA bomb that went off outside the Army Recruiting Centre. On the Friday night, me and a mate went to see the Stranglers at the De Mont. We raced to the bar, bought four pints, then got evacuated due to a bomb scare. We ended up drinking the beer outside, then went to the pub.

We saw them a couple of weeks later on March 15 at the rescheduled date. They were great.

THE EVERLY BROTHERS & DUANE EDDY
13 MAY 1991

BARRY ROBINSON
I've seen the Everlys at least three or four times. At this show, after a pounding 'Lucille', Don was gasping for breath. I was near a front row on the balcony to the right of the stage and shouted, 'You never grow old with rock and roll!' He looked up at me and said, 'I agree with that!' An old friend rang me next day saying, 'Was that you who shouted out last night?'

JOHN STRETTON
My love affair with the De Mont drew to a close. My working near London was a severe obstacle, but another factor was the emergence of punk. Definitely not my scene! But Duane Eddy and the Everly Brothers lit up the De Mont for me one more time, and I can die happy from seeing the rare sight of him singing with the Everlys in one of the closing songs of the show. Cherished memories indeed.

SUEDE
31 JANUARY 1995

CARL LIQUORISH
This was a great gig on the *Dog Man Star* tour. I remember buying the ticket late for a band that I knew little about – I did that for Genesis in '73 – knowing that the venue would bring out a great performance in them and make me a fan. I managed to sneak in on the back row of the balcony. They really had the place jumping. Brett Anderson is a woefully underrated front man in my opinion

KEVIN HEWICK

I was there with my then partner, Claire. Because she was pregnant, we sat in the balcony rather than down the front. During Suede's set she felt our daughter kick for the first time! Suede had black and white films projected behind them that effectively reflected the haunting quality of the *Dog Man Star* album. Teenage guitar wonder Richard Oakes had recently replaced Bernard Butler. He seemed totally confident in his new role. Support was the excellent and rather underrated Goya Dress featuring Astrid Williamson.

THE STONE ROSES
7 DECEMBER 1995

ALAN ROBERTS

I remember this gig well – not for the performance but for the epic football match, organised by bassist Mani, inside the venue where the punters would stand! Also, I remember they had the greatest drum stool ever, which a roadie kindly let me sit on to play the kit. It had a speaker built in, so that every time you kicked the bass drum it felt like a kick in the balls.

STEREOPHONICS
23 APRIL 1999

ALAN ROBERTS

After a fine performance from the band, we started taking down and loading. There was a lull in the loading bay, so I thought I'd roll myself a cigarette. I had no matches so I asked a guy who was sitting on a flight case for a light with my prison-regulation skinny Old Holborn cig in my mouth. 'I'm not lighting that,' said the guy who then pulled out a huge joint, 'but I'll share this with you'. We went on to chat about stuff while we shared a smoke until the cases resumed rolling towards us. So I thanked him and moved on.

'You lucky so-and-so,' a colleague later remarked in the back of the truck. 'You just shared a joint with Mr. Nice', AKA the drug smuggler Howard Marks!

GOIN' DOWN DE MONT: A PEOPLE'S HISTORY

BILLY BRAGG
25 JULY 2000

RICHARD HOUGHTON
I went with my sister, and the venue was set out with large round tables at which gig-goers were sat. It was an odd set up, but we met Billy afterwards and he explained that while he couldn't sell out the De Mont if it had been a normal standing crowd – the next biggest venue in Leicester was too small, hence the cabaret-style layout. I'm not sure it worked.

My other memory of this gig is that a woman had her camera with her. She offered to take a picture of me and Billy, which I was quite excited about being a big Bragg fan. This was the pre-digital age and the woman said she would get the photos developed and then post the pic of me with Billy on to me, so I gave her my address. Three weeks later, I got a letter from the woman, but no accompanying photo. The processing lab that was developing her film had managed to lose it.

THE OSMONDS
13 MARCH 2006

MICK BROWN
Working backstage can be great fun, soul destroying and hard work all in one day!

Everything a band needs to put on a show is toured in trucks. Some bands set will fit into one small van, others may need three or even four 40 foot trailers. A typical band load in will need ten local crew, supplied by the venue, to tip the truck and wheel the flight cases, etc. onto the stage and then to assist the touring band's crew to put the show together. Generally, this can take four to five hours to put in and two hours to take it out. It is usually a slick operation.

The Osmonds toured one 40 foot truck, which was loaded to the back doors and to the ceiling; every inch of space was used and the first row to be unloaded was about 30 motors used for the rigging. The pack was ridiculously heavy and difficult to unload and, at the end of the night, it was even harder to restack them as they were the last thing on the truck. The one saving grace was that the band and crew were very nice and very apologetic!

THIN LIZZY
22 NOVEMBER 2007

MICK BROWN
I worked at the De Montfort Hall for over 15 years, and I was the runner for the bands that came through. A runner is basically someone with local knowledge that can arrange laundry, buy food, drive the band to and from the hotel, etc.

One of my first gigs was for Thin Lizzy, and I met them at the hotel in the morning and brought them to the hall and then to various meetings and press interviews. They were all very nice and they had a new American tour manager with them who was keen, to say the least. He was quite protective of the band, and the band were not that fussed and more used to doing things their own way, being old hands and used to it.

I was instructed that, at the end of the gig, the van should be at the side of the stage exit, with the engine running to take the band back to the hotel. This was duly done and in true rock and roll style, the band came off stage with towels, got into the car and off we went.

Halfway down Lancaster Road, very close to the venue, I heard them muttering and saying how disappointed they were that there were no fans waiting for signatures and photos. I explained that there were, in fact, hundreds of fans waiting at the stage door but that the tour manager had insisted that the band left immediately. The band were furious. I offered to turn round but they pointed out that it would look stupid, so off we went back the hotel in total silence. The tour manager was sacked that night!

GOIN' DOWN DE MONT: A PEOPLE'S HISTORY

MOTÖRHEAD
11 NOVEMBER 2008

MICK BROWN

Motörhead were regular visitors to the De Mont, and I had the privilege of being their runner three times. The days were always very busy, fetching and carrying and finding things that the band needed – mainly strings, fags and alcohol. Lemmy was very easy to please. If he had cigarettes, Jack Daniels and a box of Kinder Surprise eggs, he was happy. He loved to spend all the time making the toys as it kept him busy and out of trouble. He also toured with a fruit machine!

As you can imagine, the band had a very heavy set, mainly PA and more sub bass boxes than is healthy. The band wanted me as their runner to source a company that would recharge CO_2 fire extinguishers, as these were to be used during the drum solo. I found an engineer who came to the hall to recharge them, but foolishly he tried to tell the Motörhead crew that it was in fact 'illegal' to discharge a fire extinguisher if there wasn't a fire. Reluctantly, he agreed to carry out the work as the touring crew agreed to start a fire during the drum solo!

Then the sound engineers fired up the PA and conducted a sub test. This involved sending a signal through the audio spectrum to test the rig. I can vividly remember the roof shaking as the sub bass kicked in; I thought the roof would fall in!

After a very stressful day being run ragged, I started to feel unwell, and by showtime I was feeling really bad. I was taken to hospital with a suspected heart attack. After tests, it was decided it was just stress-related and thankfully not heart-related. By the time I was released from hospital the band had gone.

KASABIAN
29 - 31 MAY 2009

TOM MEIGHAN, KASABIAN

My great memory of the De Mont was when we played there in the early days of Kasabian and I wore a vintage Leicester City shirt. I will never forget it – there was so much love and admiration because we were in our hometown, and it was extra special.

Then, eight years later, the De Mont was our dressing room when we played a sold-out gig on Vicky Park. That was surreal. Things had moved on a lot.

NICK MEE

I bought one of Serge Pizzorno's guitars from him just before the De Mont gigs. Tom Meighan and Rick Graham, his roadie, brought it to my house to hand it over; Tom was a bit of a livewire but very pleasant. He sorted passes for me, my daughter and her friend for the show on the 29th. My German shepherd Jess liked Tom, too!

Tom Meighan of Kasabian (left) with Frankie Mee

Before the gig I got to have a look at all the touring gear courtesy of Rick. Serge's gear included a good few Rickenbackers and a couple of guitars that I was told were Noel Gallagher's. The crowd were wild! I had a post-gig pass but only Chris Edwards appeared after, as far as I know. He lived across the road from me on Knighton Church Road, Leicester. Not a very talkative fella!

FRANKIE MEE

All I can remember was that we were at the front and we had a brilliant time. It was an excellent gig. People surrounding us were super friendly. When Tom threw his bottle of water out to the crowd, my friend Tara and another bloke both grabbed it, and he willingly gave it to Tara. He seemed very nice. Cups of water being handed backwards to make sure everyone was hydrated.

GOIN' DOWN DE MONT: A PEOPLE'S HISTORY

MOTÖRHEAD
18 NOVEMBER 2010

NICK MEE

Knowing from a previous visit how much he liked collecting war memorabilia, I popped round to the stage door and got straight into Lemmy's dressing room. I gave him the war stuff and he poured me a large bourbon. We then had a bizarre conversation about the anatomy of the skull and nephrology! Lemmy was the perfect gent and told me to position myself behind the mixing desk on the edge of the stage and enjoy myself.

Nick Mee met Lemmy from Motörhead in 2010 and blagged a backstage pass

MADNESS
4 DECEMBER 2010

MICK BROWN

Madness have been to the hall several times and are a fantastic live band.

I was their runner and took them to and from their hotel several times and arranged a haircut for Suggs. At about 4.30pm, their manager asked me to take them back to the hotel and liaise with them to bring them back for the show. Halfway to the hotel, the band asked me to take them to a traditional quiet pub, not the hotel. I took them to the Shakespeare's Head, which was close to the Holiday Inn where they were staying, and agreed to fetch them at 7.45pm.

The manager asked if they were dropped, and I explained that they'd decided to go to the pub instead; he was not happy, but I had no choice. I can't argue with the band. I fetched them after and, as expected, most were well-oiled and 'show ready'.

During the first number, the saxophonist walked to the front of the stage and attempted to swing on one of the upright lighting trusses, believing it to be screwed down. It wasn't, and he ended up falling off the stage into the security pit and smashing his mouth and saxophone. He ended up at the hospital for stitches, and I got the blame for taking him to the pub!

SHOWADDYWADDY
13 AUGUST 2011

DAVE BARTRAM, SHOWADDYWADDY
On a personal note, my final performance in the grounds of the De Mont in 2011 will live with me forever, when on a glorious sunny August afternoon the band took to the stage at the city's own mini-Glastonbury event, known as *Summer Sundae*. I took my hometown bow before a delirious, not to mention extraordinarily tuneful crowd, who mouthed the lyrics to pretty much every tune, providing me with a stirring swansong.

CHASE & STATUS
16 SEPTEMBER 2011

MICK BROWN
We had the fantastic Chase and Status come to the hall. They are a dubstep/drum and bass collective. The bass during the show was so low that the lighting in the balcony ceiling started to fall out and we had to have stewards with cardboard boxes collecting the debris during the show! Give them a listen if you've never heard them.

THIN LIZZY
23 JANUARY 2012

MICK BROWN

The next time I ran for Thin Lizzy was a few years after their 2007 show, and I was flattered that Scotty Gorham remembered me and the incident with the tour manager. He was a great man; very funny and easy to talk to. I remember we drove through endless traffic jams as there were major roadworks in the city. I moaned about the roads, and he moaned about LA and the problems out there with the roads.

At the end of the night, he said that most runners asked about guitar picks, string gauges, etc. but I was 'the most fucking miserable runner he'd ever met', that it was fantastic that he'd found someone that hated the roadworks as much as him, and that he'd really enjoyed my company!

MOTÖRHEAD
11 NOVEMBER 2012

MICK BROWN

The next time I worked for Motörhead came four years after I had worked for them and been taken to the hospital. They trooped in off the tour bus through stage door. I was standing outside at the time as they all filed by. Lemmy walked by, clad in his trademark trench coat and hat, and turned to me and said, 'I thought you were fucking dead', and without waiting for my answer, disappeared. At least he remembered me!

MARK SMITH

Altered Images (Clare Grogan, mmmm) in May 1982 was one of the loudest gigs I'd heard until Motörhead in 2012, and I was even in the very back row of the hall for that one. Lemmy was not best pleased when there was a power outage because of all the smoke onstage.

GOIN' DOWN DE MONT: A PEOPLE'S HISTORY

PALOMA FAITH
12 FEBRUARY 2013

MICK BROWN
I was the runner for Paloma Faith several times and on one occasion she wanted to go to a shop at Fosse Park. I took her and her manager, and started to drive. After a minute or so, the manager asked if I could talk a bit about Leicester and point our places of interest, etc. I gave what I considered to be a very informative and entertaining talk. When we arrived at Fosse Park, Paloma turned to her manager and said, 'Tell that bloke to shut up on the way back. He ain't stopped all the way here!' How rude!

MARILLION
28 - 30 APRIL 2017

CHRIS WRIGHT
This was the 2017 Marillion Weekend and my wife fixed up with Phil Brown (the band's front-of-house sound engineer, famous for his pre-gig on stage rant to the audience to watch rather than film on their phones) to ask the band to give me a shout out for my 60th birthday (knowing that is something they don't often do). Anyway, I got the shout out, and then h, Steve Hogarth, went on to tell the story (for the first time) of how he'd had three years taken off his age when he joined the band. He finally publicly admitted his true age (60). He still refers to that evening at some gigs.

This was also the first time that finger-lights came out for 'Go'. Treasured memories

JOAN AVRIL RICHES
After we did the finger-lights, I was in the hallway and this lovely young boy started talking to me. He asked if I was having fun and how much he had enjoyed the lights. He was so nice that I gave him all mine as he only had two. It turns out he was h's little boy.

I am often mistaken for Lucy Jordache, Marillion's manager, especially at the De Montfort, and have had many fans express their gratitude and love of the band to me. After a while, I just accepted their words and answered as Lucy. Lucy thinks it's great and funny and now introduces me as her twin!

ORCHESTRAL MANOEUVRES IN THE DARK
5 NOVEMBER 2017

MASON UNDERWOOD

My earliest memory of OMD involved a TV ad for a *Ministry of Sound* '80s compilation, using the melody from 'Enola Gay'. I instantly liked it. My mum seemed to get excited too, and we nipped to HMV to pick up some CDs. OMD's music quickly became the soundtrack to my brother and I playing in the back garden as Mum blared them from our windows. A decade or so later, studying at Guildford's Academy of Contemporary Music, at the end of each trimester, Mum picked me up and we'd drive back to Leicester for the holiday. On one such drive, our selection of music included a greatest hits compilation. That's when I rediscovered OMD. 'Walking on the Milky Way' stood out. Lyrics about getting older seemed rather pertinent to me in my early twenties.

I treated Mum to see OMD live, which was brilliant. Andy looked directly at me during the chorus of 'So in Love', giving me a look of utter bewilderment. I'm not totally sure why, but I suspect it's because I'm not 40, as a woman next to me made a point of mentioning.

DAVID HANSON

Almost 40 years before, I was listening to *Architecture & Morality* in my bedroom. Fast forward to 2017. After a quick chat with the wife, two tickets were booked. We arrived way too early and made our way to Row D, Seats 37 and 38, in an almost empty hall. After the support and obligatory dash for the men's room, I was back and my 38-year dream was fulfilled. From the intro and 'Ghost Star' through to 'Messages' and our request, 'The New Stone Age,' could this get any better? Then 'Joan of Arc' and 'Maid of Orleans', and a 50-something man was almost losing it. I could feel the bottom lip start to go and a tear in my eye.

CHRIS INNS

I took my 26-year-old William for his first OMD experience. He was introduced to OMD as a baby, bouncing in his static walker, hanging from my lounge doorframe. En route to the gig, he said, 'Do they do 'Tesla Girls'?' Leaving the De Montfort Hall he said, 'Dad, they are good, aren't they? And they can sing.' I gave him a big smile, and said, 'Yes, son.'

MARILLION
26 – 28 APRIL 2019

TAMARA JAMES

I fell in love with the band Marillion in 1985 with the release of *Misplaced Childhood*. After a 33-year-long hiatus, I reconnected with the band at a performance in Durham, North Carolina. I scoured the internet after that to learn everything I could about them during my long absence. I discovered that, every other year, they perform Marillion Weekends, which are three-day concerts given in various cities around the world. I decided there was no better place to see this event than the De Montfort Hall, a relatively short distance from the Marillion birthplace of Aylesbury but a long way

Marillion's Front Row Club

Finger-lights at a Marillion show in 2019

from Clarksville, Virginia. So, my husband and I flew to the UK in April 2019 and spent the night in Leicester before the kickoff to the weekend.

The next morning, we decided to walk to the De Montfort Hall to get our wristbands, which would allow us to access the venue all three nights of the event. We were amazed to see people were already in line at 10am – the first show didn't start until about 7pm! We chatted with our fellow fans and learned this is a thing – The Front Row Club, a group of people who religiously line up early for Marillion shows to make sure they get a spot in the front row. (I didn't get it at the time, but I do now!) We shook our heads, got our wristbands and continued exploring the university campus and Leicester.

The three nights at the De Montfort Hall were everything I expected and more. The most special moment was the last night, when all of the fans (who were provided with finger-lights by another generous fan) turned on the lights at one point during the song 'This Train is My Life'. The entire venue shone with thousands of tiny coloured lights. It was magical. I looked all around at my fellow fans and felt such happiness to be part of something so special.

Up on stage, I could see the band smiling with surprise and delight. It was at that moment I realised what it meant to be part of the Marillion family. The De Montfort Hall will always be special to me for these cherished memories and for being the place of my first Marillion Weekend.

CYNTHIA SILVA

My beloved boy Pedro went with us to the 2019 Leicester Weekend. We stayed at the Belmont where Pedro made friends with Ian Mosley. Ian never spoke to me. But the moment we walked in the Belmont, Ian was there. His eyes lit up when he met Pedro, and he had a treat in his pocket ready to make friends. Pedro loved his friend Ian. After the shows, I would

Cynthia's dog Pedro is gone but not forgotten

Above & right: The Hollies (2009)

Left: Fran Healy of Travis (2016)

Right: Tom Caplin of Keane (2019)

Richard Thompson (2017)

Jake Bugg (2017)

Father John Misty (2019)

Guy Garvey of Elbow (2017)

Steve Hackett (2021)

Photos - Paul Smith

go back to the hotel to take him out. Pedro would run in the hotel to find Ian, who always had dog treats in his pocket. I will never forget how sweet this man was to my little boy.

We lost Pedro in 2020. But Marillion gave him a Gone but Not Forgotten award. He was the best doggie.

THE HUMAN LEAGUE
4 NOVEMBER 2019

MICK BROWN
The Human League know how to put on a show. One of their tours had the stage covered in pristine white carpet. All the crew had to wear overshoes, and no cases could be wheeled onto the stage once the carpet was down, which of course meant carrying very heavy decking and staging across the stage and building it without marking the carpet. I was the runner for the Human League several times. They were all lovely and gave me a signed programme and t-shirt as I was working for them on my birthday!

THE STRANGLERS
25 FEBRUARY 2022

BAZ WARNE, THE STRANGLERS
This is a beautiful old theatre, and a first for me. JJ seems to recall the band playing here decades ago, and indeed, this is only the second time the band have played Leicester since I joined… the first being at the O2 just down the road a few tours ago.

When I was a kid and beginning to read the music press of the day and taking notice of touring bands and all that starry-eyed, wonderful stuff, this gig was always on the circuit… everybody played here for years, and I always wondered what it would be like to play a venue like this. Funny how some things just stick in your head.

And so, here we are. The place is buzzing and as we arrive at the Hall, I can hear The Ruts tearing into their final stretch, so I step sidestage to have a look. They're so tight and well drilled... they really do make it look effortless. I have a look out through the curtain beside me and can see the place is rammed. The Ruts finish with a huge rush of adrenalin as they always do and leave the stage to thunderous applause... job done.

We take to the stage half an hour later to the same huge roar, and quickly settle into the gig. I think we play really well, but afterwards JJ confesses to it being his worst show of the tour. 'I fucked up in every single song tonight.'

We always go on about how we're our own worst critics, and he's no different. You want to give your very best, but we're a live living breathing band, and things, of course, don't always go smoothly. I have to confess, though, I think he's being a little hard on himself. I have him loud and proud in my ear monitors and didn't hear any of the mistakes he's talking about. Jim says the same. 'Dunno what you're on about... you sounded fine to me.'

It's nice to know though that we still care very much about what we do. I think tonight is a triumph, and I tell the crowd as much at the end. Another really good gig, and I'm chuffed that on a personal level, I finally got to play such a lovely famous old place.

NICK MASON'S SAUCERFUL OF SECRETS
1 MARCH 2022

RICH BARTON

This was my most recent outing to De Mont. I only went because I got the tickets from an old friend who couldn't go due to Covid reasons. I was very grateful. Nick made a few quips about

Nick Mason in 2022

Photo - Paul Smith

mobile phone lights keeping the 'old chaps on stage awake!' The sound and lights were amazing. They played a full, note-perfect rendition of 'Echoes' and many Syd Barrett tunes, including 'Interstellar Overdrive'. And Gary Kemp's (of Spandau Ballet – who would have thought?) guitar and vocals were excellent.

The old place still produces magic for me – 50 years on!

Nick Mason and Gary Kemp in 2022 playing with Nick Mason's Saucerful of Secrets

Photo - Paul Smith

Photo - Rich Barton

AFTERWORD

Now approaching its eleventh decade of existence, the 'temporary' De Montfort Hall endures, no longer at the forefront of rock music evolution as it was from the Sixties to the Eighties but still staying true to the venue's original vision and catering to the diverse demands of Leicester's entertainment-going public. But how much longer it will endure, and whether rock music will endure alongside it as tastes and leisure habits evolve, remains to be seen.

As I write, the Leicester City Council has announced it will allow Leicester City Football Club to go ahead with its plans to build a 6,000-capacity indoor arena adjacent to the King Power stadium. Rather than spelling the De Mont's demise, I believe that a new, larger venue in the city would once again give Leicester a full range of venue sizes to compete with its Midlands rivals. This, in turn, will keep Leicester on the touring map and enable the De Mont to retain its reputation as one of the country's leading mid-sized venues for the foreseeable future.

That means the De Mont will continue to produce stories for years to come. And like the ones that appear in this book, I am optimistic they will continue to be funny, colourful, and as profound as the story of that teenager on a chair, experiencing a transcendent moment in the middle of a vibrant, life-affirming audience.

GOIN' DOWN DE MONT: A PEOPLE'S HISTORY

DE MONTFORT HALL DISCOGRAPHY

This discography only lists legitimate commercial releases of songs known to have been recorded at Leicester's De Montfort Hall.

ARTIST: Be Bop Deluxe

RECORDING DATE: 12 February 1977

SONGS: Introduction – Blimps/In the Air Age/Fair Exchange/Piece of Mine/Sister Seagull/Mill Street Junction/Ships in the Night/Swansong/Maid in Heaven/Shine/Adventures in a Yorkshire Landscape/Bill Nelson's Introduction/Twilight Capers/Modern Music Suite (Modern Music/Dancing in the Moonlight (All Alone)/Honeymoon on Mars/Lost in the Neon World/Dance of the Uncle Sam Humanoids/Modern Music [Reprise])/Forbidden Lovers/Terminal Street/Blazing Apostles

RELEASE: Several unidentified songs from this show were recorded and released on the album *Live! In the Air Age* (Harvest, SHVL 816) (1977)

The entire show was eventually released as a part of the *Live! In the Air Age* reissue 14-CD/DVD box set (Esoteric Recordings PECLEC 162760) (2021)

ARTIST: Bellowhead

RECORDING DATE: 19 November 2015

SONGS: Moon Kittens/Roll Alabama/Betsy Baker/Jack Lintel/Fine Sally/Old Dun Cow/Thousands or More/Lillibulero/Black Beetle Pies/The Wife of Usher's Well/What's the Life of a Man?/Gosport Nancy/The March Past/Greenwood Side/Let Her Run/Let Union Be/Rosemary Lane/Haul Away/Roll the Woodpile Down/London Town/New York Girls/Frogs' Legs and Dragons' Teeth/Down Where the Drunkards Roll

RELEASE: Released as a DVD as a part of the *Bellowhead Live: Farewell Tour* 2-CD/DVD package (Navigator Records, NAVIGATOR095X) (2016)

GOIN' DOWN DE MONT: A PEOPLE'S HISTORY

ARTIST: Bob Dylan

RECORDING DATE: 2 May 1965

SONGS: The Times They Are A-Changin'/To Ramona/Gates Of Eden/If You Gotta Go, Go Now/It's Alright, Ma (I'm Only Bleeding)/Love Minus Zero-No Limit/Mr. Tambourine Man/Talkin' World War III Blues/Don't Think Twice, It's All Right/With God on Our Side/She Belongs to Me/It Ain't Me, Babe /*The Lonesome Death of Hattie Carroll/All I Really Want to Do/It's All Over Now, Baby Blue/**It Takes a Lot to Laugh, It Takes a Train to Cry

RELEASE: Released as a digital download as part of the 18-CD edition of *The Cutting Edge 1965-1966: The Bootleg Series Volume 12* (Columbia, 88875124402I8) (2015)

*Also released and **released exclusively as part of the 2-DVD edition of *Bob Dylan: Don't Look Back – 65 Tour Deluxe Edition* (Columbia, 82876832139) (2007)

ARTIST: Bob Dylan

RECORDING DATE: 15 May 1966

SONGS: She Belongs to Me/Fourth Time Around/Visions of Johanna/It's All Over Now, Baby Blue/Desolation Row/Just Like A Woman/Mr. Tambourine Man/Tell Me, Momma/I Don't Believe You (She Acts Like We Never Have Met)/Baby, Let Me Follow You Down/Just Like Tom Thumb's Blues/Leopard-Skin Pill-Box Hat/One Too Many Mornings/Ballad of a Thin Man/Like a Rolling Stone

RELEASE: Released as part of the 36-CD *Bob Dylan – The 1966 Live Recordings* (Columbia, 889853581924) (2016)

GOIN' DOWN DE MONT: A PEOPLE'S HISTORY

ARTIST: Hawkwind
RECORDING DATE: 29 September 1977
SONGS: *Robot/*High Rise/**Quark, Strangeness and Charm/**Masters of the Universe/**Spirit of the Age/**Sonic Attack/***Welcome to the Future
RELEASE: *Released on the album *PXR5* (Charisma, CDS 4016) (1977)
**and ***released on the album *The Weird Tapes No. 2 - Hawkwind Live/Hawklord's Studio* (Hawkwind Records, HAWKVP7CD) (2000) and the album *Live – Sonic Attack* (Secret Records, SECDD010) (2010)
** also released on the album *Best of Live* (Secret Records, SECLP191) (2018)

ARTIST: Rory Gallagher
RECORDING DATE: 19 April 1978
SONGS: Garbage Man/Roberta
RELEASE: Released on the album *BBC Sessions* (RCA, Capo 701) (1999)

ARTIST: Gallagher & Lyle
RECORDING DATE: 2 February 1977
SONGS: I Wanna Stay With You/Breakaway/Love on the Airwaves/Runaway/Stay Young/The Greatest Australian Dream/Every Little Teardrop/Head Talk/If I Needed Someone/I Believe in You/Heart on My Sleeve/When I'm Dead and Gone
RELEASE: Released on the album *Live at the De Montfort Hall Leicester 1977* (The Store for Music, SJPCD602) (2019)

ARTIST: Genesis
RECORDING DATE: 25 February 1973
SONGS: Watcher of the Skies/Get 'em Out by Friday/Musical Box/The Knife
RELEASE: Released on the album *Genesis Live* (Charisma CLASS 1) (1973)

GOIN' DE MONT: A PEOPLE'S HISTORY

ARTIST: Marillion
RECORDING DATE: 5 March 1984
SONGS: Forgotten Sons/Garden Party/Market Square Heroes/*Chelsea Monday
RELEASE: Released on the album *Real to Reel* (EMI, EG 2603031) (1984)
*Released on the Japanese album *The Thieving Magpie (La Gazza Ladra)* (EMI, TOCP-67793·94) (2005)

ARTIST: Marillion
RECORDING DATE: 24 April 1990
SONGS: Backstage/The King of Sunset Town/Slainte Mhath/Easter/Uninvited Guest/Warm Wet Circles/That Time of the Night (The Short Straw)/Holloway Girl/Berlin/Seasons End/Hooks In You/The Space.../Kayleigh/Lavender/Heart of Lothian/Incommunicado/After Me/Market Square Heroes
RELEASE: Released as the second DVD of the 2-DVD package *From Stoke Row To Ipanema: A Year In The Life June 89 - July 90* (Sony, DVSS249751100) (2003)
Also released as part of the 8-CD box set *Marillion: The Official Bootleg Series Vol. 2* (EMI, 50999 6 32521 2 5) (2010)

ARTIST: Marillion
RECORDING DATE: 28 April 2017
SONGS: Faith
RELEASE: Released on the album *The Gold: Best Of Convention 2017* (Racket Records, Racket 61) (2017)

ARTIST: Marillion
RECORDING DATE: 29 April 2017
SONGS: The Leavers
RELEASE: Released on the album *The Gold: Best Of Convention 2017* (Racket Records, Racket 61) (2017)

GOIN' DOWN DE MONT: A PEOPLE'S HISTORY

ARTIST: Marillion
RECORDING DATE: 26 April 2019
SONGS: The King of Sunset Town/The Bell in the Sea/The Uninvited Guest/Seasons End/Splintering Heart/This Town/The Rakes Progress/100 Nights/Holidays in Eden/Dry Land/Cover My Eyes (Pain and Heaven)/Bridge/Living with the Big Lie/Runaway/The Hollow Man/Brave/Gazpacho/Cannibal Surf Babe/King
RELEASE: Released as disc 2 of the 2-DVD/Blu Ray package *Distant Lights* (Racket Records, Racket 11680) (2022)

Also released as discs 3 & 4 of the 4-CD package *Distant Lights* (Racket Records, Racket 68) (2022)

ARTIST: Marillion
RECORDING DATE: 28 April 2019
SONGS: This Train Is My Life
RELEASE: Released as a bonus track on the 4-CD package *Distant Lights* (Racket Records, Racket 68) (2022)

ARTIST: Bill Nelson's Red Noise
RECORDING DATE: 8 March 1979
SONGS: Stay Young/Out of Touch
RELEASE: Released on the 12" EP *Revolt Into Style* (12 HAR 5183) (1979)

ARTIST: The Sensational Alex Harvey Band
RECORDING DATE: 22 May 1976
SONGS: Fanfare/The Faith Healer/*Tomahawk Kid/*Isobel Goudie/Amos Moses/Vambo/*Boston Tea Party/*Dance to Your Daddy/*Framed/Delilah
RELEASE: Released on the album *British Tour '76* (Major League Productions, MLP07CD) (2004)

*Also released on *Alex Harvey: The Last of the Teenage Idols* box set (Universal Music Catalogue, 536212-0) (2016)

GOIN' DOWN DE MONT: A PEOPLE'S HISTORY

ARTIST: Steeleye Span

RECORDING DATE: 11 February 1978

SONGS: Galtee Farmer/Awake Awake/The Saucy Sailor/The Black Freighter/Hunting the Wren/Sweep, Chimney Sweep/The Duke of Athols Highlanders/Walter Bulwer's Polka/Cam Ye O'er Frae France/The Boar's Head/Seventeen Come Sunday/Rave On

RELEASE: Released on the album *Live at the De Montfort Hall Leicester England 1977* (The Store for Music, SJPCD601) (2019)

ARTIST: Streetwalkers

RECORDING DATE: 26 February 1977

SONGS: Walking on Waters/Crazy Charade/Me an' Me Horse an' Me Rum/Mama Was Mad/Chilli-Con-Carne/My Friend the Sun/Burlesque/Toenail Draggin'/Run for Cover/Can't Come In

RELEASE: Released on the album *Rip it Up at the DeMontfort* (Mystic, MYS CD 212) (2013)

ARTIST: Don Van Vliet (aka Captain Beefheart) and The Magic Band

RECORDING DATE: 30 March 1972

SONGS: Hair Pie Bake III/Smoking Rio/Hair Pie Bake III/The Mascara Snake/The Mascara Fake/The Mascara For God's Sake/When It Blows It Stacks/Click Clack/Grow Fins/Band Intro/Hobo Chang Ba/I'm Gonna Booglarize You Baby/Old Black Snake/Peon/Abba Zabba/Woe Is Uh Me Bop/Alice in Blunderland/Spitball Scalped a Baby/More/Bass Solo/My Human Gets Me Blues/Steal Softly Through Snow/Saxophone Solo/Saxophone and Drums Medley/Band Introduction/Golden Birdies

RELEASE: Released on the album *Don Van Vliet And The Magic Band: Rough, Raw And Amazing Live At Leicester De Montfort Hall 1972* (Dandelion Records, OZIT DAN LP 8024) (2015)

GOIN' DOWN DE MONT: A PEOPLE'S HISTORY

ARTIST: Wishbone Ash
RECORDING DATE: 14 June 1971
SONGS: Where Were You Tomorrow
RELEASE: Released on the album *Pilgrimage* (MCA, MDKS 8004) (1971)

ARTIST: Bill Wyman's Rhythm Kings
RECORDING DATE: 27 June 2000
SONGS: I'm Ready/Jump, Jive and Wail
RELEASE: Released on the album *Bootleg Kings Ride Again* (Ripple Records, RIPCD 002) (2001)
Also released on *Kings of Rhythm Vol 1: Jump Jive & Wail* box set (Edsel, EDSB 4029) (2016)

GOIN' DOWN DE MONT: A PEOPLE'S HISTORY

ROCK CONCERTS AT LEICESTER'S DE MONTFORT HALL 1957-2023

The following is as accurate as possible.
Please contact Bruce Pegg at demontstories@gmail.com for any additions or corrections, which will be included in any future editions of this book.

1957
January 3: Pat Boone **February 3:** Tommy Steele & The Steelmen **March 13:** The Platters/Ronnie Aldrich & The Squadronaires (*The Squadronaires featured Cliff Townshend, Pete Townsend's father*) **May 16:** Frankie Lymon/Terry Lightfoot & His Jazzmen/Chas McDevitt Skiffle Group with Nancy Whiskey/Billy Anthony **September 8:** Terry Dene & The Dene-Aces/The Squadronaires

1958
January 7: Josephine Douglas/Freddie Mills/John Barry & His Seven/The Five Dallas Boys/Cab Kaye & His Quintet/Adam Faith/Kerry Martin/The Vernons Girls/Pete Murray (*Compere*) **March 6:** Paul Anka **16:** Buddy Holly/Gary Miller/Tanner Sisters/Ronnie Keene's Orchestra/Des O'Connor (*Compere*) **June 16:** The Treniers/Chas McDevitt Skiffle Group/Hedley Ward Trio/Terry Wayne (*Jerry Lee Lewis was supposed to headline but left the tour after three dates due to the media outrage surrounding his marriage to his 13-year-old cousin*) **26:** Tommy Steele **October 5:** Marty Wilde & His Wildcats/Chas McDevitt & His Skiffle Group/Vince Eager & His Vagabonds/The John Barry Seven/Sonny Roy (*Compere*) **14:** The Kalin Twins/Eddie Calvert/Cliff Richard & The Drifters (*Not the American Drifters, but the band that went on to become The Shadows*)/The Most Brothers/The Londonaires/Tony Marsh (*Compere*)

1959
March 12: Connie Francis/Tony Dalli/George Martin/Pierre Bel/Nino/Dennis Spicer/Hedley Ward Trio/Six Flying De Pauls/The John Tiller Girls/Harold Collins & His Orchestra **December 6:** Cliff Richard & The Shadows/Peter Elliott/Roy Young/The Kingpins/Al Saxon/Bill & Brett Landis/The Tommy Allen Group/Tony March (*Compere*)

GOIN' DOWN DE MONT: A PEOPLE'S HISTORY

1960
January 24: The Platters **February 18**: Eddie Cochran/Gene Vincent/Vince Eager/Viscounts/Tony Sheriden/The Wildcats/The Beat Boys **March 20:** Bobby Darin/Duane Eddy & The Rebels/Clyde McPhatter/Emile Ford & The Checkmates/Bob Miller & The Millermen/Alan Field (*Compere*) **April 17:** The Everly Brothers/The Crickets/Five Dallas Boys/Cherry Wainer & Don Storer/Lance Fortune/Danny Hunter/Flee-Rekkers/Freddy Lloyd Five/Tony Marsh (*Compere*) **May 25:** Conway Twitty/Freddie Cannon/Johnnie Preston/Wee Willie Harris/Chris Wayne & The Echoes/Tony Crombie/Don Arden (*Compere*) (*Don Arden, who also promoted the show and many others in the 60s, was Sharon Osbourne's father*) **September 2:** The Shadows/Chas McDevitt & Shirley Douglas/Frank Ifield/Michael Cox/Paul Beattie & The Beats/Dave Reid (*Compere*) **November 6:** Cliff Richard & The Shadows/Cherry Wainer/The Kingpins/Bill & Brett Landis/Sally Kelly/The Billy Woods Five/Reg Thompson (*Compere*)

1961
February 13: Cliff Richard & The Shadows/The Brook Brothers/Chas McDevitt & Shirley Douglas/The Hunters/Dave Sampson/Norman Vaughan (*Compere*) **March 5:** Billy Fury/Mark Wynter/Tommy Bruce/Joe Brown/Nelson Keene/Duffy Power/The Four Kestrels/Johnny Gentle/Georgie Flame/The Valentine Girls/New Orleans Rockers **September 17:** Johnny Kidd & the Pirates/Joe Brown/The Flee-Rekkers/Danny Rivers/Vince Eager/Michael Cox/Nero & the Gladiators/Don Munday (*Compere*) **24:** Cliff Richard & The Shadows

1962
February 17: Bobby Vee/Tony Orlando/Clarence Frogman Henry/The Springfields/Suzy Cope/Jimmy Crawford/Billy Burden/The Ravens **25:** Billy Fury & The Tornados/John Leyton/Eden Kane/Karl Denver Trio/Shane Fenton & The Fentones/Joe Brown & The Bruvvers/Jackie Lynton/Ricky Stevens/Peter Jay & The Jaywalkers/Don Munday (*Compere*) (*Shane Fenton went on to find fame in the Seventies as Alvin Stardust*) **March 8:** Cliff Richard & The Shadows/Dallas Boys/Patti Brooks/The Trebletones/The Two Tones/Tony Marsh (*Compere*)

GOIN' DOWN DE MONT: A PEOPLE'S HISTORY

April 11 Brenda Lee/Gene Vincent/Rory Blackwell & The Blackjacks/ Nero & The Gladiators/Sounds Incorporated/Bob Bain (*Compere*) **24:** Gary US Bonds/Johnny Burnette/Gene McDaniels/The Flee Rekkers/Four Kestrels/Rolly Daniels/Condors/Danny Rivers/Mark Wynter (*Compere*) **30:** Jerry Lee Lewis/Johnny Kidd & The Pirates/The Viscounts/Vince Eager/The Echoes/Mark Eden/Danny Storm/Buddy Britten/Dave Reid (*Compere*) **September 16:** Chubby Checker/Brook Brothers/Kestrels/Susan Singer/Chas McDevitt & Shirley Douglas/ Gary Edwards Combo/Red Price & His Orchestra/Bob Bain (*Compere*) **30:** Dion/Del Shannon/Buzz Clifford/Joe Brown/The Allisons/ Wallace & Duvall/Suzy Cope/Peppi/The New York Twisters
October 7: Billy Fury/Karl Denver Trio/Joe Brown/Marty Wilde/ Mike Sarne/Jimmy Justice/Mark Wynter/Peter Jay & The Jay Walkers/ Al Paige (*Compere*) **November 4:** Bobby Vee/The Crickets/Ronnie Carroll/Russ Sainty & The Nu Notes/Frank Kelly & The Hunters/ Johnny de Little/Frank Berry (*Compere*) **December 9:** Adam Faith/ Gene Vincent/The Roulettes/The Trebletones/Chance Gordon/Peter Gordeno/Dave Reid (*Compere*)

1963
January 27: Frank Ifield/The Springfields/The Lana Sisters/Jackie Trent/Tommy Wallis & Beryl/Ted Taylor Four/Alan Field (*Compere*) **February 17:** Brian Hyland/Little Eva/The Brook Brothers/The Chariots/Johnny Temple/Rhythm & Blues Quintet plus One/ Dave Reid (*Compere*) **March 23:** Cliff Richard & The Shadows/Patsy Ann Noble/The Vernons Girls/Alan Randall/The Trebletones/Frank Berry (*Compere*) **31** Chris Montez/Tommy Roe/The Beatles/Viscounts/ Terry Young Six/Debbie Lee/Tony Marsh (*Compere*)
April 21: Del Shannon/Johnny Tillotson/The Springfields/Kenny Lynch/Peppi/The Eagles/Jerry Stevens (*Compere*) **May 20:** Ray Charles **September 22:** Billy J. Kramer & The Dakotas/Tommy Roe/The Fourmost/Heinz & The Saints/The Dennisons/Johnny Sandon & The Remo Four/Chris Carlson (*Compere*) **October 6:** Gerry & The Pacemakers/Del Shannon/Jet Harris & Tony Meehan/The Bachelors/ Duffy Power/Cilla Black/Bryan Burdon/Blue Diamonds
November 10: Billy Fury/Joe Brown/Karl Denver Trio/The

Tornados/Marty Wilde/Daryl Quest/Dickie Pride/The Ramblers/Cilla Black (possibly)/Larry Burns (*Compere*) **17:** Freddie & the Dreamers/Dusty Springfield/Brian Poole & the Tremeloes/The Searchers/Dave Berry & The Cruisers/Susan Singer/Tony Marsh (*Compere*) **24:** Duane Eddy/The Shirelles/Gene Vincent/Gary US Bonds/Carter-Lewis & The Southerners/Mickie Most/Flintstones/Roof-Raisers/Ray Cameron (*Compere*) **December 1:** The Beatles/The Brook Brothers/The Kestrels/Peter Jay & The Jaywalkers/The Vernons Girls/Rhythm & Blues Quartet/Frank Berry (*Compere*)

1964

January 26: The Ronettes/The Rolling Stones/Dave Berry & The Cruisers/Marty Wilde & The Wildcats/Swinging Blue Jeans/The Cheynes/Al Paige (*Compere*) **February 9:** The Rolling Stones/John Layton (possibly)/Mike Sarne/The Swinging Blue Jeans/Don Spencer/Billy Boyle/Mike Berry/Billie Davis/Jet Harris/The Paramounts **21** Adam Faith/Sandy Shaw/The Barron Knights/The Paramounts/Roulettes/Patrick Kerr/Freddie Earl (Compere) **March 1:** Gerry & The Pacemakers/Ben E. King/The Fourmost/Tommy Quickly/The Dennisons/Sounds Incorporated/Jimmy Tarbuck (*Compere*) **8:** Joe Brown & The Bruvvers/The Crystals/Johnny Kidd & The Pirates/Heinz & The Saints/Daryl Quist/Mike Preston/Manfred Mann/Kevin Kirk/Al Paige (*Compere*) **22:** The Searchers/Bobby Vee/Dusty Springfield/Big Dee Irwin/The Echoes/Suzy Cope/Alan Davison/Tomy Marsh (*Compere*) **31:** Dave Clark Five/The Hollies/The Kinks/Mark Wynter/The Trebletones/The Mojos/Frank Berry (*Compere*) **April 26:** Roy Orbison/Freddie & The Dreamers/Wayne Fotana & The Mindbenders/Tony Sheriden & The Bobby Patrick Big Six/Chris Sandford & The Coronets/Ezz Reco & The Launchers/The Federals/Glen Mason (*Compere*) **May 24:** Chuck Berry/Carl Perkins/Brenda Lee/The Animals/Kingsize Taylor/The Other Two/Nashville Teens/Larry Burns (*Compere*) **June 14:** Dave Clark Five/The Applejacks/Millie & The Five Embers/The Worryin' Kind/The Quiet Five featuring Patrick Danes/The Falling Leaves/Adrian Kildare (*Compere*) **July 8:** Ray Charles **26:** The Rolling Stones/Gene Vincent/Marty Wilde/The Barron Knights/Julie Grant **October 4:** Bill Haley & His Comets/

GOIN' DOWN DE MONT: A PEOPLE'S HISTORY

Manfred Mann/Nashville Teens/Rocking Berries/Bobby Patrick Big Six/Untamed Four/Bob Bain (*Compere*) **10:** The Beatles/Mary Wells/Tommy Quickly/The Remo Four/Sounds Incorporated/Michael Haslam/The Rustiks/Bob Bain (*Compere*) **24:** Animals/Carl Perkins/Tommy Tucker/Elkie Brooks/Plebs/Nashville Teens/Quotations/Ray Cameron (*Compere*) **November 1:** The Hollies/The Dixie Cups/Heinz & The Wild Boys/Jess Conrad/The Tornados/The Hi-Fis/Wayne Gibson & The Dynamic Sounds/Larry Burns (*Compere*) **15:** The Honeycombs/Millie/Lulu & The Luvvers/Applejacks/Darryl Quist/Beat Merchants/Puppets/Freddie Earl (*Compere*) **29:** Cilla Black/The Fourmost/Cliff Bennett & The Rebel Rousers/A Band of Angels/Pete & Geoff Stringfellow/Sounds Incorporated

1965
February 28: Roy Orbison/Rockin' Berries/Marianne Faithful/Cliff Bennet & The Rebel Rousers/The Untamed/The Three Quarters/John Mark/Frank Berry (*Compere*) **March 21:** Billy Fury/The Gamblers/The John Barry Seven & Orchestra/Bobby Pattinson **April 18:** The Kinks/The Pretty Things/Tommy Quickly/The Walker Brothers/Micky Finn/he Remo Four/Sounds Incorporated **May 2:** Bob Dylan (*see discography*) **9:** Tom Jones/Marianne Faithful/The Who **16:** Donovan/Wayne Fontana & the Mindbenders/Unit Four + 2/New Faces/John L. Watson & The Hummelflugs/Chris Carlsen (*Compere*) **September 18:** Peter, Paul, & Mary **26:** Cliff Richard & The Shadows **October 10:** The Everly Brothers/Cilla Black/Billy J. Kramer & The Dakotas/Paddy, Klaus & Gibson/The Marionettes/Lionel Blair Kick Dancers/The Alan Elsdon Band/Pete Brady (*Compere*) **13:** The Rolling Stones/Spencer Davis Group/Unit Four + 2/Checkmates/Charles Dickens & The Habits/Ray Cameron (*Compere*) **November 10:** Gene Pitney/Rockin' Berries/Lulu & The Luvvers/Peter & Gordon/Mike Cotton Sound/The Quiet Five/Syd & Eddie (*Comperes*) **December 5:** The Walker Brothers/Small Faces

1966
March 21: PJ Proby/The Searchers/The Action/Thane Russal & Three/Shelley/Shirly & Johnnie/Tony Marsh (*Compere*) **April 10:** Roy Orbison/

Walker Brothers/Lulu & The Luvvers/The Marionettes/Kim D & The Del Five/The Quotations/Ray Cameron (*Compere*) **22:** The Small Faces/The Truth/Alan Field/Crispian St. Peters/The Overlanders/Fran and Alan/The Puppets **May 6:** The Kinks/The Merseys/The Sean Buckley Set/Dave Dee, Dozy, Beaky, Mick & Tich/Goldie **15:** Bob Dylan (*see discography*) **October 2:** The Walker Brothers/The Troggs/Dave Dee, Dozy, Beaky, Mick & Tich/Clodagh Rogers/The Montanas/The Quotations/Don Crockett (*Compere*) **November 9:** The Beach Boys/Lulu/David & Jonathan/Sounds Incorporated/The Golden Brass

1967
February 5: Four Tops/Madeline Bell/The Remo Four/The Merseys
March 19: The Hollies/Spencer Davis Group/Paul Jones/The Tremeloes/Richard Kent Style/The Young Idea/Dave Butler (*Compere*)
April 2: Roy Orbison/Small Faces/Paul & Barry Ryan/Jeff Beck Group/Settlers/Sonny Childe & The TNT/Robb Storme Group/The Settlers/Ray Cameron (*Compere*) **16:** The Walker Brothers/Cat Stevens/Engelbert Humperdinck/Jimi Hendrix/Californians/Quotations/Nick Jones (*Compere*) **October 1:** The Shadows/Roy Castle/Jane Sutton/The Trebletones **15:** Traffic/Tomorrow with Keith West/The Flower Pot Men/Vanilla Fudge/Art/Jeffrey Lenner (*Compere*) **22:** American Folk Blues Festival - Sonny Terry & Brownie McGhee/Son House/Muddy Waters/Skip James/Bukka White/Little Walter/Hound Dog Taylor/Dillard Crume/Odie Payne/Koko Taylor/Joe Boyd (*Compere*) (*Joe Boyd went on to produce Pink Floyd's first single and produced/managed many English folk-rock acts of the early Seventies*)

1968
April 14: The Kinks/The Herd/The Tremeloes/Gary Walker & The Rain/Ola & The Janglers/The Life 'N Soul/Ray Cameron (*Compere*) **21:** Gene Pitney/Amen Corner/Status Quo/Simon Dupree & The Big Sound /Lucas & The Mike Cotton Sound/Don Partridge/Tony Branson (*Compere*) **July 18:** Tim Hardin/Family **October 27:** American Folk-Blues Festival '68 - John Lee Hooker/T-Bone Walker/Big Joe Williams/Jimmy Reed/Curtis Jones/Eddie Taylor Blues Band
December 5: Pentangle

GOIN' DOWN DE MONT: A PEOPLE'S HISTORY

1969
March 2: Gene Pitney/The Marmalade/Joe Cocker & The Grease Band/The Iveys/Lucas & The Mike Cotton Sounds/Mike Quinn (*Compere*) **13:** Led Zeppelin/Ferris Wheel/Decoys **23:** Incredible String Band **October 23:** Jethro Tull/Savoy Brown/Terry Reid **24:** Pentangle **November 2:** American Folk, Blues & Gospel Festival '69 - Albert King/John Lee Hooker/Champion Jack Dupree/Otis Spann **9:** John Mayall **December 4:** Family/Emily Muff

1970
February 24: The Nice **26:** Incredible String Band **March 9:** Colosseum/Taste **18:** Fotheringay/The Humblebums/Nick Drake **April 13:** Fairport Convention/Mandragon **30:** Taj Mahal/Rare Bird **May 11:** Deep Purple **17:** John Mayall **28:** Family/Emily Muff **September 14:** Taste/Stone the Crows/Jake Holmes **21:** Derek & the Dominoes/Brett Marvin & The Thunderbolts **23:** Canned Heat/The Groundhogs **27:** Emerson, Lake & Palmer **28:** Jethro Tull/Tir Na Nog/Procol Harum **November 1:** American Folk, Blues & Gospel Festival '70 - Sonny Terry & Brownie McGhee/Sister Rosetta Tharpe/Bukka White/Champion Jack Dupree/Willie Dixon's Chicago Blues All Stars with Shakey Horton/Lee Jackson/Clifton James/Lafayette Leak **December 1:** Family/America

1971
February 15: Quintessence **23:** Free/Amazing Blondel **25** Deep Purple/Hardin & York **March 1:** Leon Russell **April 7:** Emerson, Lake & Palmer **21:** The Strawbs/Brake & Crane **May 16:** Rory Gallagher **23:** King Crimson **25:** T. Rex **June 13:** Caravan/Barclay James Harvest **14:** Wishbone Ash/Stackridge/Glencoe (*see discography*) **29:** Curved Air **July 4:** The Who **September 14:** Cat Stevens **19:** Deep Purple/Bullet **20:** Traffic/Paul Rogers' Peace **22:** Ten Years After/Keith Christmas/Supertramp **30:** Yes/Jonathan Swift **October 3:** Incredible String Band **18:** King Crimson **November 1:** Family/America **7:** Buffy St. Marie/Loudon Wainwright III **8:** T. Rex **24:** Elton John/England Dan & John Ford Coley **30:** Fairport Convention

GOIN' DOWN DE MONT: A PEOPLE'S HISTORY

1972
January 27: Wishbone Ash/Glencoe **February 1:** Black Sabbath **10:** Pink Floyd **14:** Free/Sutherland Brothers **27:** The Moody Blues **March 9:** Rory Gallagher/Nazareth **14:** Jethro Tull **30:** Captain Beefheart (*see discography*) **May 8:** Electric Light Orchestra/Colin Blunstone/F.F.Z. **21:** The Beach Boys **June 18:** Uriah Heep/Mike Maran **September 14:** Deep Purple/Glencoe **19:** Free **20:** Traffic **October 11:** Jackson Heights/Magna Carta/Jefferson **October 12:** Lindisfarne/Genesis/Rab Noakes **30:** Soft Machine/Mick Greenwood **November 6:** Ten Years After **21:** Emerson, Lake & Palmer

1973
January 29: Family/Linda Lewis **February 1:** Darryl Way's Wolf **February 15:** Steeleye Span **22:** Rory Gallagher **25:** Genesis/String Driven Thing (*see discography*) **March 1:** Elton John/Longdancer **15:** The Temptations/Jr Walker & the All Stars **19:** Roxy Music/Sharks **April 1:** The Supremes **2:** Status Quo/Byzantium **May 6:** Focus **24:** Jo'Burg Hawk/Capability Brown **June June 11:** David Bowie **16:** Sweet **25:** Roy Wood's Wizzard **26:** Gary Glitter **July 16:** Hawkwind **September 13:** Family/Philip Goodhand-Tait (*Family's farewell tour*) **20:** The Kinks **24:** Argent/Glencoe **27:** Lou Reed **30:** Steeleye Span **October 4:** Lindisfarne/Capability Brown/Darien Spirit **7:** Man **11:** Darryl Way's Wolf **18:** Genesis/Ron Geesin **29:** Nazareth/Silverhead **30:** Roxy Music/Leo Sayer **November 22:** Rory Gallagher/Strider **26:** Yes **December 17:** Black Sabbath/Highway

1974
January 2: Hawkwind **13:** Beck, Bogert, and Appice **February 13:** Ralph McTell **27:** T. Rex **March 11:** Stackridge **22:** Mott the Hoople **April 10:** The Strawbs **21:** Mud/Sweet Sensation **28:** Mick Ronson **29:** Gong/Hatfield and the North **June 25:** Showaddywaddy **September 15:** Leo Sayer **October 1-2:** Roxy Music/Jess Roden Band **3:** Sensational Alex Harvey Band/Slack Alice **7:** Wishbone Ash **29:** Uriah Heep/Peter Frampton **November 4:** Sparks/Pilot **26:** Golden Earring/Lynyrd Skynyrd **December 1:** Tangerine Dream **9:** Steeleye Span

GOIN' DOWN DE MONT: A PEOPLE'S HISTORY

1975

January 27: Supertramp/Gallagher & Lyle/Chris de Burgh
30: Hawkwind **February 3:** Baker-Gurvitz Army/Strife **25:** Naughty Rythms Tour - Dr. Feelgood, Chilli Willie & The Red Hot Peppers, Kokomo
26: Al Stewart/Brinsley Schwarz **March 2:** Neil Sedaka
5: Stackridge/Shepstone & Dibbens **11:** Edgar Broughton Band
23: 10cc/Fancy **24:** Steve Harley & Cockney Rebel **26:** Showaddywaddy
April 21: Rory Gallagher **24-25:** Yes/Gryphon **May 8-9:** Status Quo/ The Pretty Things **20:** Sensational Alex Harvey Band **29:** Don McLean **30:** Roy Harper/Trigger/Headstone **July 24:** Duane Eddy
August 1: Chris Farlow **September 12:** Showaddywaddy/Arrows
21: Budgie/Hobo **24:** Argent **25:** Greenslade/A.J. Weber **30:** David Essex
October 2: Barclay James Harvest/Café Society **15:** Dr. Feelgood/G.T. Moore & the Reggae Guitars **17:** Melanie **27:** Steeleye Span/Cajun Moon
December 1: Supertramp/Joan Armatrading **3:** Uriah Heep/Tim Rose
4: Nazareth/Snafu

1976

February 1: Commander Cody & His Lost Planet Airmen/Barry "The Fish" Melton **12 & 13:** 10cc/Chas & Dave **21:** Emmylou Harris
March 15: Man **16:** Diana Ross **April 4:** Stylistics/Brook Benton
10: Camel/Hazzard & Barnes **20:** Rick Wakeman **May 5:** Elton John **10:** Budgie/Dirty Tricks **22:** Sensational Alex Harvey Band/Pat Travers *(see discography)* **June 3:** Dr. Hook/Unicorn **July 1:** Curved Air
September 1: Rainbow/Stretch **22:** Manfred Mann's Earthband/ Racing Cars **28:** Be Bop Deluxe/Burlesque **October 4:** Hawkwind/ Tiger **23:** Dr. Feelgood **25:** Thin Lizzy/Clover **28:** Barclay James Harvest/Easy Street **29:** Showaddywaddy/The Great British Invention
November 7: Santana **8:** Wishbone Ash **22:** Steeleye Span/Martin Simpson **December 12:** Man

1977

January 21-22: Genesis *(two shows on the 21st at 6:30 & 9:15)*
February 2: Gallagher & Lyle *(see discography)* **3:** Bryan Ferry
12: Be Bop Deluxe/Steve Gibbons Band *(see discography)* **14:** Lynyrd Skynyrd/Clover **15:** Rory Gallagher/Joe O'Donnell Band

26: Streetwalkers/Foster Brothers (*see discography*) **March 1:** Uriah Heep/Woody Woodmansey's U-Boat **28:** Graham Parker & The Rumour **April 20:** Eric Clapton/Ronnie Lane **May 14:** Ralph McTell **28:** The Clash/The Buzzcocks/Subway Sect/The Slits **June 9:** Ian Hunter/The Vibrators **July 21:** Boxer/Crawler/Moon **September 21:** Peter Gabriel/Nona Hendryx **22:** Caravan/Nova **26:** Dr. Feelgood/Mink DeVille **28:** Camel/Andy Desmond **29:** Hawkwind/Bethnal (*see discography*) **October 2:** Barclay James Harvest/Paul Brett **3:** The Stranglers **24:** Wishbone Ash/The Motors **28:** Steve Hillage/Glenn Phillips **November 28:** The Damned/The Dead Boys **December 1:** Uriah Heep/Fury **5:** Thin Lizzy/Radiators From Space **7:** Showaddywaddy **12:** David Essex/The Alessi Brothers

1978

February 7: Judas Priest/English Assassin **11:** Steeleye Span/Tannahill Weavers (*see discography*) **13:** Rush/Tyla Gang **16:** Be Bop Deluxe/John Cooper Clarke **22:** Adverts/Wayne County & the Electric Chairs/Cortinas/Staa Marx/Suburban Studs/Depressions/Bethnal
March 12: Eddie & the Hot Rods/Squeeze **28:** Elvis Costello & The Attractions **April 9:** The Adverts/Groundation/Cool Notes
19: Rory Gallagher/Joe O'Donnell (*see discography*) **May 31:** Black Sabbath/Van Halen **June 2:** Blue Öyster Cult/Japan **5:** Ian Dury and the Blockheads **19:** UFO/Marsailles **September 10:** The Shadows **15:** Camel/Soft Machine/Michael Chapman **22:** Renaissance/Iain Matthews **26:** Tom Robinson Band **October 1:** Dr Feelgood **9:** Jasper Carrott **15:** Barclay James Harvest/Michael Moore **23:** Hawklords/The Softies **31** Wishbone Ash
November 2: The Jam **3:** Judas Priest/Lee Hart **7:** Sham 69/The Cimarons **20:** The Clash/The Slits **21:** Whitesnake/Magnum **26:** Talking Heads/The Newmatics **27:** Lindisfarne/Chris Rea/Mike Eliot **December 19:** Showaddywaddy

1979

January 22: Elvis Costello & The Attractions **30:** Nazareth/Blazer Blazer **February 5:** UFO/Liar **7:** Rory Gallagher **27:** Steve Hillage/Telephone **March 8:** Bill Nelson's Red Noise (*see discography*)

26: Graham Parker & The Rumour **27:** Journey/Pat Travers
April 5: Thin Lizzy/The Vipers **8:** Motörhead/Girlschool
May 2: Roxy Music/The Tourists **21:** Judas Priest/Marseilles
29: The Tubes/Squeeze **July 16-17:** Ian Dury and the Blockheads
September 9: The Police/Fashion **18:** Siouxsie & the Banshees/
The Cure **26:** Tom Robinson Band **October 11:** Gillan/Randy
California/Samson **15:** Whitesnake/Marseilles **21:** Camel **30:** Steve
Hillage/Trevor Rabin **31:** Gallagher & Lyle/Judie Tzuke **November
5:** 2-Tone Tour (The Specials/Madness/The Selecter/Dexy's Midnight
Runners) **9:** AC-DC/Def Leppard **12:** Blue Öyster Cult/Magnum **14:**
Motörhead/Saxon
22: The Damned/Victim/The Misfits **27:** Ten Years Later/The Bogey
Boys **December 2:** Dr. Feelgood **2:** Hawkwind/Tipper
10: Lindisfarne/Chas & Dave/Mike Eliot **18-19:** The Jam/The Vapours
27: Blondie/Whirlwind

1980

January 16: The Clash **17:** The Ramones **21:** UFO/Girl **29:** Wishbone
Ash/The Dukes **February 10:** Uriah Heep/Girlschool
24: Peter Gabriel/Random Hold **March 1:** The Tourists/45s (*Rescheduled
from 25 February*) **13:** Judas Priest/Iron Maiden **14:** Nazareth/Saxon
30: Gerry Rafferty/Richard & Linda Thompson **April 8:** Sammy
Hagar/Riot **15:** Genesis **27:** Def Leppard/Magnum/Quartz
May 1: Judie Tzuke/Graduate **12:** Sky **18:** Thin Lizzy **23:** Joe Jackson
26: Black Sabbath/Shakin' Street **June 2:** Whitesnake/G-Force
17: Iron Maiden/Praying Mantis **20:** Van Halen/Lucifer's Friend
21: Rush **23:** Steve Hackett **September 24:** David Essex
28: Gillan/Quartz/White Spirit **29:** Ozzy Osbourne/Budgie
October 3: UFO/Fist **6:** Rory Gallagher/Rage **7:** The Tourists
12: Pretenders/Tenpole Tudor/The Moondogs **16:** Scorpions/Blackfoot
20-21: AC-DC/The Starfighters **24:** Hawkwind
November 10: Triumph **11:** Sad Café **12 & 13:** The Jam
17-18: Motörhead/Weapon **25-25:** Yes **26:** Elkie Brooks/Richard
Digence **December 2:** Hazel O'Connor/Duran Duran
4: Saxon/Limelight **15:** Jon Anderson/Claire Hamill **20:** Ian Dury & the
Blockheads **21:** Madness

1981
January 9: Boomtown Rats **February 22:** Siouxsie & the Banshees **March 2:** Camel **3:** The Stranglers **7:** Duran Duran **9:** Slade **12:** Krokus/More **22:** Elvis Costello & The Attractions **April 6:** Steeleye Span/Paul Goodman **15:** Orchestral Manoeuvres in the Dark **28:** Girlschool/A II Z **May 6:** The Kinks/The AK Band **7:** The Au Pairs **11:** The Cure **22:** Toyah **23:** Barclay James Harvest/John Benns **24:** Wishbone Ash/Nicky Moore Band **June 9:** Judie Tzuke/Woolly Wolstenholme's Maestoso **22:** Kraftwerk **23:** Robert Palmer **25:** The Tubes/The Spangs **28:** Apocalypse Now Tour - Discharge/The Exploited/Chron Gen/Anti-Pasti **September 15:** Michael Schenker Group/The Starfighters **16:** David Essex **28:** The Shadows **October 2:** Hawkwind **9:** Saxon **10:** Dr. Hook/Sundance **12:** Sad Café **November 9:** Judas Priest **15:** Orchestral Manoeuvres in the Dark **17:** Shakin' Stevens **December 3:** Squeeze **9:** The Pretenders **11:** Gillan/Budgie/Nightwing **12:** Duran Duran **14:** Thin Lizzy (*Rescheduled from 10 November*)

1982
January 18: UFO/Girl **February 11:** UB 40 **15:** Krokus **March 5:** Iron Maiden/The Rods **14:** 10cc **22-23:** The Jam **25:** Slade **April 7-8:** Motörhead/Tank **16:** Blackfoot **22:** Scorpions/Wolf (*Rescheduled from 1 March*) **23:** Judie Tzuke **29:** Thin Lizzy/Lone Wolf **May 22:** Girlschool/Raven **26:** Camel **27:** Altered Images/Vic Goddard/Subway Sect **June 6:** Toyah **July 20:** The Clash (*Rescheduled from 3 May*) **September 21:** Saxon **24:** Elvis Costello & The Attractions **October 14:** Kid Creole & The Coconuts **20:** Kim Wilde **22:** Michael Schenker Group **November 1:** Japan **7:** Hawkwind **8:** Duran Duran **December 3:** U2 **4:** Michael Schenker Group **12:** Simple Minds **13:** Dire Straits **14:** Gillan/Spider: **23:** Whitesnake

1983
January 30: Echo and the Bunnymen **February 17:** Thin Lizzy/Mama's Boys **March 27:** UFO/Socrates **April 10:** Joan Armatrading **15:** Orchestral Manoeuvres in the Dark **28:** Clarence "Frogman" Henry **May 6:** Iron Maiden/Grand Prix **22:** Eric Clapton **June 21:** Bauhaus

30: Motörhead/Anvil **October 6:** Gary Numan **24:** Kiss **27:** Michael Schenker Group/Wildfire **31:** Elvis Costello & The Attractions/The TKO Horns/Afrodiziak **November 8:** Dio **10:** Ozzy Osbourne/Heavy Pettin' **16:** Eurythmics **December 12:** Culture Club/Swinging Laurels (*two shows*) **14:** Lindisfarne **20:** Judas Priest/Quiet Riot **21:** Robert Plant **23:** Showaddywaddy/The Tremeloes

1984
January 7: The Pretenders **February 8:** Tina Turner **12:** The Clash **26:** Saxon **March 5:** Marillion/Pendragon (*see discography*) **11:** Hawkwind **12:** Simple Minds/Silent Running **18:** The Smiths/The Telephone Boxes **April 9:** The Kinks/The Truth **June 26:** Van Morrison **20:** Siouxsie & the Banshees **July 2:** Big Country **September 17:** Echo and the Bunnymen/Let's Active **19:** Orchestral Manoeuvres in the Dark **20:** Iron Maiden/Waysted **October 2:** Dio/Queensryche **10:** Kiss/Bon Jovi **17:** Elvis Costello & The Attractions/The Pogues **November 15:** Meat Loaf **27:** Gary Numan **December 10:** Lindisfarne

1985
January 17: Meat Loaf **March 15:** Frankie Goes to Hollywood **April 1:** The Smiths/James **May 7:** Rick Wakeman/Claire Hammill **30:** The Cult **June 21:** The Damned/The Fuzztones/Dr. & the Medics **July 28:** Freddie & the Dreamers **September 28:** Gary Numan **30:** Gary Moore **October 3:** Spear of Destiny **14:** Siouxsie & the Banshees **November 4:** Madness **5:** Bo Diddley **18:** The Cult **19:** UFO/Pallas **26:** Magnum **28:** Hawkwind/Dumpy's Rusty Nuts **29:** The Everly Brothers **December 3:** The Style Council

1986
January 28: Red Wedge - Billy Bragg/Paul Weller/The Communards **29:** Marillion/Beltane Fire **30:** Feargal Sharkey **February 25:** Clannad **March 3:** Ozzy Osbourne/Chrome Molly **May 23:** The Cramps **27:** Black Sabbath **July 2:** Big Country/Balaam and the Angel **September 14:** Leicester Aid - The Sweet/Laurel Aitken/Chrome Molly/Abandoned Babies/Eugene **October 14:** Iron Maiden/Paul Samson's Empire **16:** Magnum/FM **November 11:** Hawkwind/The

Babysitters **14:** Big Audio Dynamite/Chiefs of Relief **23:** Bon Jovi/FM **28:** Status Quo **December 9:** Lindisfarne

1987
January 27: Nik Kershaw **March 14:** The Pogues **30:** The Cult/Crazy Head **April 5:** Simply Red **28:** Barclay James Harvest **September 14:** Gary Numan **15:** Def Leppard/Tesla **19:** Squeeze **November 2:** Anthrax/Testament **December 16:** Lindisfarne

1988
February 8: INXS/Voice of the Beehive **23:** The Pogues **March 21:** Magnum/Kingdom Come**April 25:** Hawkwind **May 10:** Saxon/Pretty Maids **June 16:** Judas Priest/Bonfire **September 15:** Siouxsie & the Banshees **October 4:** Gary Numan **November 17:** Cinderella/Little Angels

1989
April 10: The Monkees **May 7:** Clannad **13:** Then Jericho **17:** R.E.M./Blue Aeroplanes **September 7:** Black Sabbath/Axxis **23:** The Stranglers **October 23:** The Wonder Stuff/The Sandkings/Ned's Atomic Dustbin **29:** Ian McCulloch **30:** Julia Fordham **November 6:** The Jesus and Mary Chain/Perfect Disaster **27:** Clannad **December 5:** Richard Marx **16:** Lindisfarne

1990
March 15: The Stranglers/Ugly as Sin (*This is the rescheduled date. The original show on 23 February was cancelled right after the support act had played due to a bomb scare.*) **April 9:** Marillion **24:** Marillion (*see discography*) **September 3:** Black Sabbath/Circus of Powe **October 2:** Iron Maiden/Wolfsbane **11:** New Model Army/Levellers **14:** Pixies/Barkmarket **15:** The Pogues **November 5:** Hawkwind **8:** Van Morrison/Georgie Fame **December 10:** Magnum/Roko **12:** Thunder/No Sweat **17:** Lindisfarne

1991
March 28: Gary Numan **May 8:** Lenny Kravitz **13:** The Everly Brothers/Duane Eddy **15:** The Beautiful South **30:** The Wedding Present/Buffalo Tom **October 8:** Morrissey/Phranc **9:** James

18: Van Morrison **November 19:** Johnny Cash **December 9:** The Pogues **14:** New Model Army

1992
March 23: The Verve/Ride/Mercury Rev **24:** Gary Numan
July 13: Crowded House **October 10:** Happy Mondays **16:** Pop Will Eat Itself **November 23:** Ned's Atomic Dustbin

1993
February 13: Van Morrison **March 30:** Jeff Healey
April 26: New Model Army **June 9:** 10cc **July 13:** INXS
September 13-14: Levellers **October 25:** Gary Numan
November 3: The Kinks

1994
The Hall was closed from January until November for the installation of the tiered seating system

1995
January 31: Suede/Goya Dress **March 1:** Chuck Berry **18:** The Prodigy
April 12: Solid Silver 60s Show - Peter Noone/Freddie & The Dreamers/Wayne Fontana & The Mindbenders/The Troggs **October 5:** Squeeze
13: Joan Armatrading **20:** The Everly Brothers **25:** The Manfreds/Peter Sarstedt **December 7:** The Stone Roses

1996
February 25: Deep Purple **April 11:** Mike & the Mechanics
May 10: Clannad **June 11:** Paul Weller **October 4:** Suede
23: Manic Street Preachers **28:** Erasure **November 14:** Skunk Anansie
16: Runrig

1997
January 28: Kula Shaker **March 23:** James/Hardbody/Silver Sun
May 12-13: Supergrass **14:** Placebo/Scafo **23:** Lightning Seeds/The Wannadies **28:** Alan Price **June 19:** The Everly Brothers **November 4:** Sleeper **20:** Black Grape/Dust Junkys

GOIN' DOWN DE MONT: A PEOPLE'S HISTORY

1998
March 4: Levellers **17:** The Searchers/Helen Shapiro/Swinging Blue Jeans
May 5: Dolly Mixture **October 15:** Gay Dad **29:** Ash/Idlewild
December 20: Slade

1999
March 19: The Hollies **April 19:** Ocean Colour Scene
23: Stereophonics/The Crocketts **October 9:** The Manfreds/Colin Bluntstone/Chris Farlowe/Alan Price **28:** The Charlatans
November 20: Elvis Costello/Steve Nieve

2000
March 8: The Searchers/Gerry & The Pacemakeers/Peter Sarstedt/ The Swinging Blue Jeans **15:** Mary Wilson/Martha Reeves/Edwin Starr **May 5:** Gene Pitney **June 27:** Bill Wyman's Rhythm Kings (*see discography*) **July 25:** Billy Bragg **October 9:** David Gray
17: The Manfreds/Alan Price/Chris Farlowe/Cliff Bennett
19: Joan Armatrading/Martyn Joseph **December 4:** Slade **11:** Levellers

2001
February 24: Ray Davies (*Storyteller show*) **April 6:** The Hothouse Flowers **10:** Peter Noone/Dave Dee, Dozy, Beaky, Mick & Tich/Dave Berry/Wayne Fontana/The Dakotas **22:** Steve Harley & Cockney Rebel
July 1: B. B. King **8:** Summer Sundae (*Lineup: https://en.wikipedia.org/ wiki/Summer_Sundae#2001_Lineup*) **October 30:** Nanci Griffith/Tom Russell **November 1:** Muse/Hundred Reasons **23:** The Bootleg Beatles

2002
February 19: Judie Tzuke **20:** Spencer Davis/The Troggs/The Yardbirds **March 15:** Billy Bragg & The Blokes **April 23:** Saw Doctors
May 12: Lambchop **30:** Petula Clark **June 25:** The Manfreds/Long John Baldry/Colin Bluntstone/Chris Farlowe **July 6-7:** Summer Sundae (*Lineup: https://en.wikipedia.org/wiki/Summer_Sundae#2002_Lineup*)
24: Paul Weller **September 22:** Morcheeba **November 1:** Level 42
December 5: Steeleye Span

GOIN' DOWN DE MONT: A PEOPLE'S HISTORY

2003
January 27: Love with Arthur Lee **31:** The Homecoming
March 4: Richard Thompson Band/Kim Richey **July 8-10:** Summer Sundae (*Lineup: https://en.wikipedia.org/wiki/Summer_Sundae#2003_Lineup*) **October 16:** The Nice **19:** The Manfreds/Alan Price/Colin Bluntstone/P. P. Arnold **20:** The Waterboys

2004
January 23: Bill Wyman's Rhythm Kings **May 18:** Ralph McTell **26:** Alvin Lee/Edgar Winter/Tony McPhee **July 7:** Bonnie Raitt **August 13-15:** Summer Sundae (*Lineup: https://en.wikipedia.org/wiki/Summer_Sundae#2004_Lineup*) **November 19:** Jools Holland **30:** Oysterband/The Handsome Family/James O'Grady/June Tabor/Christine Collister

2005
February 20: Crosby & Nash **28:** Embrace **April 14:** The Australian Pink Floyd Show **May 23:** Elvis Costello & The Imposters
June 3: Todd Rundgren/Joe Jackson/Ethel **14:** Ben Folds (Rescheduled from 12 November 2004) **June 17-19:** The Big Session Festival (*Lineup: https://www.last.fm/festival/834523+Big+Session+2005*) **July 9:** Van Der Graaf Generator **August 12-14:** Summer Sundae (*Lineup: https://en.wikipedia.org/wiki/Summer_Sundae#2005_Lineup*) **September 26:** Ray Davies/John Riley **October 14:** Kate Rusby **November 11:** Jamie Callum **14:** Motörhead **15-16:** Jools Holland **30:** Blondie

2006
January 30: John Cale **February 16:** Sparks **March 13:** The Osmonds **April 26:** The Australian Pink Floyd Show **June 16-18:** The Big Session Festival **July 22:** Glen Campbell **August 11-13:** Summer Sundae (*Lineup: https://en.wikipedia.org/wiki/Summer_Sundae#2006_Lineup*) **October 16:** Embrace **November 13:** Motörhead **16:** Jools Holland **December 5-6:** Kasabian

2007
April 4: The Australian Pink Floyd Show **27:** James Taylor
June 14-16: The Big Session Festival (*Lineup: https://www.last.fm/festival/210166+Big+Session+Festival*)

August 10-12 Summer Sundae (*Lineup: https://en.wikipedia.org/wiki/Summer_Sundae#2007_line-up*) **November 14:** The Temptations/Ron Tyson/The Four Tops **22:** Thin Lizzy/Diamond Head **26-27:** Jools Holland

2008
February 11: Richard Hawley/Vincent Vincent & The Villains **13:** Paramore/Kids In Glass Houses/New Found Glory/Conditions **March 7:** Natasha Bedingfield **May 19:** Paul Weller/The Troubadors **June 9:** Petula Clark **13-15** The Big Session Festival (*Lineup: https://www.last.fm/festival/473842+The+Big+Session+Festival/lineup*) **August 8-10** Summer Sundae (*Lineup: https://en.wikipedia.org/wiki/Summer_Sundae#2008_line-up*) **November 11:** Motörhead

2009
March 11: The Hollies **May 29-31:** Kasabian **June 19-21**: The Big Session Festival **August 14-16**: Summer Sundae (*Lineup: https://en.wikipedia.org/wiki/Summer_Sundae#2009_line-up*) **December 3:** The Bootleg Beatles **5:** Bill Wyman's Rhythm Kings **11:** Steeleye Span

2010
January 27: Joe Brown **February 4:** Lostprophets **March 4:** Sgt. Pepper's Lonely Hearts Club Show **11:** Jerry Dammers' Spatial A.K.A. Orchestra **12:** Call Up the Groups - Barron Knights/Fortunes/The Tremeloes/Marmalade **April 19:** Joan Armatrading **21:** From The Jam **May 7:** Glenn Campbell **20:** The Solid Silver 60s Show - Dave Berry/Mike Pender/Brian Poole/Peter Sarstedt **21:** One Night of Queen **June 18-20:** The Big Session Festival **July 3:** Robert Cray **August 13-15:** Summer Sundae (*Lineup: https://en.wikipedia.org/wiki/Summer_Sundae#2010_line-up*) **November 18:** Motörhead **December 4:** Madness **15:** James **18:** The Human League

2011
May 9: Brit Floyd **August 12-14:** Summer Sundae (*Lineup: https://en.wikipedia.org/wiki/Summer_Sundae#2011_line-up*) **September 16:** Adele **October 7:** Chase & Status **11:** Bill Wyman's Rhythm Kings **November 17:** June Tabor and Oysterband **December 15:** The Bootleg Beatles

GOIN' DOWN DE MONT: A PEOPLE'S HISTORY

2012
January 23: Thin Lizzy **April 17:** The Osmonds
August 17-19: Summer Sundae (*Lineup: https://en.wikipedia.org/wiki/Summer_Sundae#2012_line-up*) **October 9:** Ray Davies **12:** Deacon Blue
November 11: Motörhead/Anthrax **December 15:** The Bootleg Beatles

2013
February 7: Fairport Convention **12:** Paloma Faith
March 15: Stereophonics **May 6:** McFly **July 3:** Rufus Wainwright
27-28 Simon Says Festival (*Lineup: https://www.efestivals.co.uk/festivals/simonsays/2013*) **November 1:** Bryan Ferry **4:** Brit Floyd **8:** Sensational 60s Experience - The Marmalade/Herman's Hermits/Chris Farlowe/Steve Ellis's Love Affair

2014
February 19: The Australian Pink Floyd Show **March 26:** Clannad/Mary Black **31:** Manic Street Preachers/Wolf Alice **May 6:** Yes
11: Ian Anderson **July 26-27:** Simon Says Festival (*Lineup: https://www.efestivals.co.uk/festivals/simonsays/2014*) **September 12:** Frank Turner
October 6: Level 42 **23:** Sixties Gold - Gerry & the Pacemakers/The Searchers/P.J. Proby/The Fortunes/Brian Poole & Chip Hawkes
November 8: Counting Crows/Lucy Rose **14:** Paloma Faith
26: Brit Floyd **28:** Human League **December 3:** Bombay Bicycle Club
6: The Bootleg Beatles

2015
February 21: Ryan Adams **March 16:** Placebo **April 19:** Mike & the Mechanics **June 22:** Elvis Costello/Larkin Poe **July 25-26:** Simon Says Festival (*Lineup: https://www.efestivals.co.uk/festivals/simonsays/2015*)
October 24: Steve Hackett **November 10:** The 1975 **19:** Bellowhead (*see discography*)

2016
February 16: Paul Carrack **March 11:** Country/Midge Ure/Nick Hayward/Curiosity Killed the Cat **May 16:** Travis/Sarah Walk
26: Adam Ant **June 4:** Uprising Festival featuring Metal 2 the Masses Final

July 23-24: Simon Says Festival (*Lineup: https://www.efestivals.co.uk/festivals/simonsays/2016*) **October: 20:** Sixties Gold - The Searchers/Brian Poole & the Tremeloes/Wayne Fontana/P.J. Proby/Gary Puckett & the Union Gap **November 8:** KT Tunstall/Braids **10:** David Essex **24:** Jools Holland

2017
March 1: Brit Floyd **3:** Paul Young/Matika/Toyah/China Crisis **16:** Elbow **21:** Thunder/Cats in Space **29:** Mike & the Mechanics **April 28-30:** Marillion (*see discography*) **May 17:** Paul Rodgers/Deborah Bonham **21:** Adam Ant **June 17:** Rick Wakeman **July 29-30:** Simon Says Festival **October 26:** Richard Thompson/Josienne Clarke & Ben Walker **29:** The Musical Box **November 5:** Orchestral Manoeuvres in the Dark **6:** Jake Bugg

2018
February 23: Paul Carrack **March 14:** Brit Floyd **April 13:** Public Service Broadcasting/Jane Weaver **26:** Barlow/KT Tunstall **May 12:** The Waterboys **June 6:** James Bay/Lily Rendle-Moore **July 11:** Levellers Acoustic **September 28:** Signed, Sealed, Delivered: A Tribute to Stevie Wonder **October 3:** The Musical Box **4:** Level 42/The Blow Monkeys **9:** Tony Hadley **12:** Sixties Gold - The Searchers/The Merseybeats/The Fortunes/Steve Ellis/Vanity Fare/P.J. Proby **13:** Bowie Experience **23:** The Proclaimers **28:** Chas & Dave **29:** Father John Misty **November 8:** Jessie J **17:** Seasick Steve **21:** The Queen Extravaganza **27:** The Australian Pink Floyd Show **28-29:** Jools Holland Rhythm & Blues Orchestra/Marc Almond **December 2:** Deacon Blue **4:** The Human League/Midge Ure

2019
January 31: Some Guys Have All the Luck: The Rod Stewart Story **February 9:** Thunder **March 3:** A Beautiful Noise: Neil Diamond Tribute **5:** Ward Thomas/Wandering Hearts **8:** Mike & the Mechanics **10:** Brit Floyd **15:** Paul Carrack **17:** Rumours of Fleetwood Mac **22:** KT Tunstall **25:** Gabriele **April 3:** Steeleye Span **24:** The Specials **26-28:** Marillion **30:** 10cc **May 3:** Richard Ashcroft **11:** UB40 **20:** The Vamps **21:** Stereophonics **24:** One Night of Queen

GOIN' DOWN DE MONT: A PEOPLE'S HISTORY

29: Howard Jones/China Crisis **31:** Manic Street Preachers **August 18:** Kaiser Chiefs/The Vaccines/The Twang **September 25:** Keane **October 2:** What's Love Got to Do With It: A Tribute to Tina Turner **8:** Midge Ure **November 1:** Sixties Gold - Herman's Hermits/The Merseybeats/Wayne Fontana & the Mindbenders/The Marmalade/Steve Ellis **4:** The Human League **8:** Steve Hackett **December 3:** The Australian Pink Floyd Show **4:** Dr. Hook (*50th anniversary tour*) **7:** The Bootleg Beatles

2020
The Hall was closed from March 2020 until September 2021 for the pandemic.

2021
September 10: Steve Hackett **October 1:** Nick Cave & Warren Ellis **3:** Fontaines DC **12:** Dr. Hook **20:** Paloma Faith **21:** Jethro Tull **27:** Kasabian **November 9:** Orchestral Manoeuvres in the Dark/Stealing Sheep **21:** Sixties Gold - The Tremeloes/Herman's Hermits/The Merseybeats/The Marmalade/P. J. Proby/Steve Ellis/Dave Berry/Mamas & Papas UK/Gerry's Pacemakers **23:** The Australian Pink Floyd Show **26:** Stereophonics **December 4:** The Bootleg Beatles

2022
February 25: The Stranglers/Ruts DC **March 1:** Texas **11:** Status Quo **April 10-11:** Paul Weller **May 1:** Nick Mason's Saucerful of Secrets **3:** Robert Cray Band **27-29:** Marillion **June 14:** Elvis Costello/Ian Prowse **15:** The Hollies (*60th Anniversary Tour*) **16:** The Drifters **September 2:** Adam Ant **October 7:** Steve Hackett **11:** 10CC/Paul Canning **18:** Blue Öyster Cult/Cats in Space **November 4:** The Proclaimers/John Bramwell **12:** Bellowhead **25:** Saxon/Diamond Head **29:** Placebo/Cruel Hearts Club **December 3:** The Bootleg Beatles

2023
February 8: The Musical Box **28:** Suzanne Vega/Sam Lee **April 6:** The Sensational 60s Experience (The Trems, The Fortunes, The Swinging Blue Jeans, Vanity Fare, Mike D'Abo) **April 22:** Mike & the Mechanics **May 5:** Fisherman's Friends **24:** Midge Ure/India Electric Co. **27-28:** Marillion **July 4:** James **October 6:** Howard Jones

Photos - Paul Smith

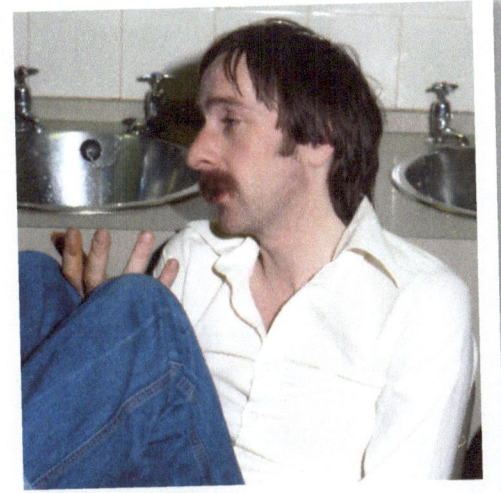

Alan Hull of Lindisfarne (1978)

Annie Lennox of the Eurythmics (1983)

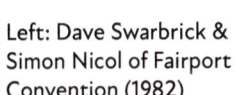

Left: Dave Swarbrick & Simon Nicol of Fairport Convention (1982)

Yes (1980)

Nils Lofgren (2015)

Left: Lindisfarne (1983)

Photos - Paul Smith

Steve Hackett (2021)

David Coverdale of Whitesnake (1980)

Photos - Paul Smith

De Mont lighting at UFO (1985)

Lee Harris playing with Nick Mason (2022)

Ian Gillan (1980)

Nick Mason (2022)

Francis Rossi of Status Quo (1984)

Marillion light up the De Mont (2019)

Photo - Alan Jones

Guy Garvey of Elbow (2017)

Edwin Hind of Virgin Dance (1983)

Francis Rossi, Guy Garvey & Edwin Hind - photos Paul Smith

De Montfort Hall, Leicester — Ticket Stubs

- **Michael Schenker** plus Guests — Thurs 15th September, 7.30 p.m., £3.50 inc. V.A.T.
- **Sammy Hagar** — Wed. Feb. 13, 7.30 p.m., Standing £2.50 (including V.A.T.)
- **The Musical Box — A Genesis Extravaganza**: An unprecedented musical feast of favourites and rarities 1970–1978 — Wed 03 Oct 2018 20:00, Right Circle, £37...
- **Steve Hackett Genesis Revisited 2019** (Kilimanjaro Live presents) — Fri 08 Nov 2019 19:..., Rear Circle, £41.00, G 27, Full Price, 4727670
- **Def Leppard** + Guests Magnum & Quartz (MCP presents) — Sunday April 27 at 7.30 p.m., Standing £2.50 (including V.A.T.), 75
- **Thin Lizzy** + Support (Adrian Hopkins presents) — Sunday May 18 at 7.30 p.m., Gallery £4.00, E 20
- **U.F.O.** + Support (Adrian Hopkins presents) — ...21 7.30 p.m., Stalls £2.75, Standing, 797
- **10CC** (In Association with Kennedy St. Artistes / Arthur Kimbrell presents) — Fri. Feb. 13 at 7.30 p.m., Stalls Standing £1.50 (including V.A.T.), 1190
- **AC/DC** (M.C.P. presents) — Mon. Oct. 26, 7.30 p.m., Stalls Standing £4.50 including VAT, 1517
- **Robert Plant** plus Special Guests (MCP & Harvey Goldsmith Entertainments presents) — Wednesday 21st December at 7.30 p.m., Standing £5.00 inc., 769
- **Judas Priest** (Harvey Goldsmith presents) — Tues. Feb. 7 at 7.30 p.m., Stalls £1.40, Standing, 876
- **Judas Priest** (Midland Concert Promotions present) — Fri. Nov. 3 at 7.30 p.m., Stalls £2.00 (including V.A.T.), Standing, 469
- **Sammy Hagar** (Straight Music presents in concert) — Wed. Feb. 13 at 7.30 p.m., Standing £2.50
- **Whitesnake** in Concert plus Support (Barry Dickins and Rod Macsween present) — Mon. June 2, 8.00 p.m., Stalls £2.50 Standing, 1188
- **Genesis** (Harvey Goldsmith by arr. with Tony Smith presents) — Fri. Jan. 21 at 6.30 p.m., Balcony £2.80 (including V.A.T.), A 53
- **Dio** plus Guests **Queensryche** (MCP by arr. with NIJI Productions & ITB presents) — Tuesday 2nd October at 7.30 p.m., Balcony £5.50 inc. V.A.T., A 78
- **The Australian Pi...** — Wed 26 Apr ..., Left Circle, £22.50

www.ingramcontent.com/pod-product-compliance
Lightning Source LLC
Chambersburg PA
CBHW040026130526
44591CB00028B/55